To
Jeevan,

With Best Wishes

Seshu

Timeless
Values

THE *Mananam* SERIES

(*Mananam*–Sanskrit for "Reflection upon the Truth")

(continued on inside back page)

Other Chinmaya Publication Series:

THE *Self-Discovery* SERIES

THE *Hindu Culture* SERIES

THE *Mananam* SERIES

Timeless Values

To the Class of 1997

Compliments of IASF and

The Chinmaya Mission of Middle Georgia

CHINMAYA PUBLICATIONS

Chinmaya Publications
Chinmaya Mission West Publications Division
Main Office
P.O. Box 129
Piercy, CA 95587, USA

Chinmaya Publications
Chinmaya Mission West Publications Division
Distribution Office
560 Bridgetown Pike
Langhorne, PA 19053, USA
Phone: (215) 396-0390   Fax: (215) 396-9710
Toll Free: 1-888-CMW-READ (1-888-269-7323)

Central Chinmaya Mission Trust
Sandeepany Sadhanalaya
Saki Vihar Road
Mumbai, India 400 072

Credits:

Series Editors: Margaret Leuverink, Br. Rajeshwar
Front cover design and inside photographs: Treehouse Digital Studio
Photograph of Thich Nhat Hanh: Courtesy of Simon Chaput

Library of Congress Catalog Card Number 96-86229

ISBN 1-880687-11-9

Contents

PART FOUR

TOWARD ETHICAL EXCELLENCE

Preface

If our lives are to be lived with any depth and meaning they need to be based upon a set of values unconditioned by time, place, or circumstance. What are these values? Vedanta philosophy teaches that the ultimate value is to realize our true nature as that Reality which is eternal happiness and peace divine. The scriptures further declare that all other values have meaning and exist as preparations for this final goal. Thus we have been given a profound reason for living a virtuous life.

We have heard about moral values such as truthfulness, compassion, and self-control. They form the basis of all religions and go to the very heart of spiritual life. But it is only when we practice and live these virtues that we come to discover their efficacy. To integrate these divine qualities into our every thought, word, and deed is true spiritual living. That is why all the great spiritual masters constantly advise, "Be good, do good, be kind and compassionate, love and serve all, and slowly move toward the final goal."

This book shows how a value-based life enhances our own well-being and that of others around us, and purifies the mind in preparation for realizing the ultimate Reality. Part One, "Eternal Principles," begins by giving an explanation of the term "values" and lists the eternal principles common to all religions. The authors state that a return to value-based living is essential for solving the problems that exist in society today.

In the first article, Swami Bhajanananda, a senior monk of the Ramakrishna Mission and former editor of *Prabuddha Bharata,* points out that values must be rooted in a clear understanding of the ultimate Reality. He also explains that yoga is the development of inner discipline, which acts as the connecting link between values and Reality.

The Vedantic Master, Swami Chinmayananda, expounds the three eternal principles of moral and ethical values in Hinduism: self-control, non-injury, and truthfulness. He explains how these principles correspond to the different layers of our personality—physical, mental, and intellectual—and that adherence to these principles is the most practical way of purifying and controlling our actions. The Buddhist author, Jack Kornfield, writes that we need to live up to our principles at a time when universal laws have almost been forgotten. These laws are the basis of conscious spiritual life and to follow and refine them leads to liberation of all beings. The Buddhist monk Thich Nhat Hanh then comments on each of the five major precepts of Buddhism in contemporary terms, showing how compassion is cultivated by living these principles.

Swami Chinmayananda begins Part Two, "Moral Refinement," by tackling a number of questions on ethics and morality. He shows how the different moods of the mind determine our ability to be morally sensitive.

John Powell, a Jesuit priest, explains how we all live in a "comfort zone," outside of which we feel threatened and insecure. He says that we must overcome our inhibitions by a process of stretching to become truly liberated and virtuous. Swami Sivananda, founder of the Divine Life Society, states that the truly moral person performs all duties with a happy and cheerful heart, accepting everything as sent by God for his own evolution. The Sufi Master Meher Baba elaborates upon a number of divine qualities which a spiritual aspirant needs to develop while performing his daily duties. He states that spiritual practice requires not only physical endurance but also "unshrinking forbearance and unassailable moral courage."

Part Three, "Reflections on Values," contains a number of personal testimonials by individuals whose lives were enriched by the practice of virtuous living. We begin with Lewis M. Andrews, an American research psychologist, who through his own practice learned that mental health and spiritual values are inseparable. Aasha Reddy, a wife and mother, writes that harmony in the home does not come about by chance, but requires effort and the close observance of a value system. Swami Vidyatmananda from the Ramakrishna Mission in France tells how he admired the two qualities of availability and positiveness, as exemplified by his teacher.

Peace Pilgrim, a contemporary American Saint who walked across the country for peace and shared with others the peace she found within herself, writes that the goal is to get to a point where our higher nature–our God-centered nature–takes over our lower self-centered nature completely. In the next article we get an idea of the genius of the American statesmen and philosopher, Benjamin Franklin, who developed a scientific approach for the cultivation of virtues.

In Part Four, "Toward Ethical Excellence," we learn more about the requirements necessary for reaching the ultimate goal. Swami Tyagananda, editor of *Vedanta Kesari* of the Ramakrishna Mission, addresses the question of what to do when our desire to live a moral life comes in conflict with the demands of our secular commitments. He says we must make a clear distinction between the essentials and nonessentials of life and learn never to compromise with our principles. Swami Chinmayananda then comments on some verses from the sixteenth chapter of the *Bhagavad Gītā,* describing certain qualities which serve as a guideline for all those who long for spiritual perfection.

Thus we see how a virtuous life helps purify the mind, preparing us for contemplation on the oneness underlying all phenomena. The practice of values which was once an effort then becomes effortless as this awareness, that we are not different from others, opens our hearts and prompts us to naturally love and serve all. This is how we create a truly ethical society. Both individual and social happiness are assured when we discover the intrinsic harmony of our higher Self.

The Editors

PART ONE

Eternal Principles

*Nothing can bring you peace
but the triumph of principles.*

Ralph Waldo Emerson

Though all religions have taught ethical precepts such as "Do not kill, do not injure, love your neighbor as yourself," and so on, none of them have given the reason why. Why should we not injure our neighbors, or love our neighbor as ourself? To these questions there was no satisfactory or conclusive answer until it was revealed by the metaphysical speculations of the Vedantic philosophers, who could not rest satisfied with mere dogmas.

The rishis said that there is one *Brahman*, who is absolute and all-pervading, and therefore infinite. There cannot be two infinities, for they would limit each other, and become finite. Also each individual soul is a part and parcel of that universal Soul, which is infinite. Therefore, by injuring his neighbor, an individual actually injures himself. This is the basic metaphysical truth underlying all ethical codes.

Swami Vivekananda

I

Values, Yoga, and Reality

by Swami Bhajanananda

Two recent events have shocked human conscience all over the world for their utter senselessness and potential danger to humanity. One is the poison gas attack on commuters in the subway system of Tokyo in March 1995 that killed a dozen people and injured more than five thousand people. The other event is the bomb blast that shattered a federal building in Oklahoma in the United States killing more than 130 people including many children in April 1995.

The poison gas attack was the work of a Japanese religious sect consisting mostly of young people. The surprising thing about this sect is that it could attract some of the most brilliant, highly educated young men to its ranks. Social scientists trying to investigate what went wrong with these smart and talented youths put the blame on the present educational system in Japan. Although rated as one of the best in the world, the Japanese educational system lacked proper value orientation, they pointed out. A *New York Times* report quoted a longtime professor of philosophy at Sophia University in Tokyo as saying, "It reflects a profound crisis in the educational system. Many Japanese students are absorbing even greater amounts of information, but they don't acquire the ability to make value judgments on basic human values, like responsibility for human life or respect for freedom of the individual."

Far more foreboding is the Oklahoma bombing. It is said to have been engineered by a fanatical paramilitary group whose members have been described by the New York City Police Commissioner as, "basically white supremacists, Christian fundamentalists, some of them totally hostile to the federal government. . . . They have been a kind of low-level infection, as it were, on the body politic." The emergence of this national network of fanatical militia men adds a new threat to civic order in a society already plagued by the collapse of family life, racism, drug addiction, juvenile gang wars, crime, and violence. Reviewing the present situation in American society, Allan Bloom, author of the well-known book *The Closing of the American Mind*, says that the "most important and most astonishing phenomenon of our time, all the more astounding in being unnoticed, is that there is now an entirely new language of good and evil, originating in an attempt to get *beyond good and evil*, and preventing us from talking with any conviction about good and evil any more. . . . The new language is that of value relativism, and it constitutes a change in our view of things moral and political as great as the one that took place when Christianity replaced Greek and Roman paganism."

More than the increase in immorality, it is the elimination of the notion of guilt from modern man's mind that Allan Bloom finds profoundly disturbing. A drastic change in modern man's concept of morality is now taking place. A form of behavior or lifestyle which had till now been regarded as an aberration or perversion is now accepted as normal and moral. For instance, thousands of men and women in Western countries cohabit without the compulsion of marriage and without any compunction. According to Barbara Dafoe Whitehead of the Institute for American Values, "there has been a shift in the social metric." At some point in the 1970's Americans changed their minds about such disruptive behavior as divorce and unwed motherhood. "What had once been regarded as hostile to children's best interests was now considered as essential to adults' happiness," says Ms. Whitehead.

About this shift in social metric an eminent conservative leftist Christopher Lasch says in his posthumous publication *The Revolt of the Elites and the Betrayal of Democracy,* "A lust for immediate gratification pervades American society from top to bottom. There is a universal concern with the self—with self-fulfillment, and, more recently, with self-esteem, slogans of a society incapable of generating a sense of civic obligation."

More than a century ago Nietzsche spoke of the need for "transvaluation of all values." Perhaps a kind of transvaluation is going on all over the world. At any rate, we need to have a fresh look at the value system that governs modern society. Every culture is in a state of equilibrium between its system of values and its system of beliefs. Science and technology have considerably altered modern man's views on Life and the universe. This has resulted in drastic changes in the system of beliefs, but the value system has not responded adequately to these changes. This is the root cause of the "crisis in values" we see in all departments of modern life. We do not propose to undertake a comprehensive study of this crisis. Our purpose here is only to offer some conceptual clarification regarding values and their relation to views on reality and social norms.

The Meaning of Values

There is a good deal of vagueness and confusion about the word "values." The well-known American psychologist Abraham Maslow writes: "However, 'values' are defined in many ways, and mean different things to different people. As a matter of fact, it is so confusing semantically that I am convinced we will soon give up this catchall word in favor of a more precise and more operational definition for each of the many submeanings that have been attached to it."[1]

Values is most commonly used as a substitute for the words

"virtues" and "morality." The latter are plainer words, and yet many people, especially politicians, seldom use them—either because of the credibility gap or because of the religious overtones of these words. So, instead of these plain words, they use the word values.

But values do not mean only virtues. One way to understand what "value" means is to distinguish values from facts. When we say that the *Bhagavad Gītā* was composed before the 3rd century B. C. or that the Taj Mahal was built by Shah Jahan, we are making a factual statement. But when we say that it was wrong on the part of Arjuna to lay down arms or that the Taj Mahal is the most beautiful building in the world, we are making a value judgment. In fact, we live in two worlds: the world of facts and the world of values. These two worlds do not always correspond to each other. Values often lead us beyond the world of facts and point to goals beyond the senses. Another way to understand what value means is to trace its origin. The term value entered philosophical thinking by way of economics. In economics it is used to mean (a) the capacity of an object to satisfy a human need or desire (this is known as value in use), or (b) money (value in exchange). It is the first meaning that is relevant here.

It is well known that man has a hierarchy of needs which provide the motivation for his behavior. According to Abraham Maslow, these needs, in ascending order, are: biological needs, security, love, esteem, knowledge, aesthetic needs, self-actualizing and transcendence.[2] Of these the lower needs connected with man's physical existence, such as the need for food, clothing, shelter, and so on are called "basic needs" or simply "needs." The needs higher to these constitute *values.*

However, values are not mere higher needs or desires. Rather, they imply what is *desirable* or *valuable.* Being desired is only a part of the meaning of valuable. Not all things that are desired are valuable, and some things that are not desired by many people today are undoubtedly valuable.

7

In the words of sociologist Clyde Kluckhohn:

> Values do not consist in desires but rather in the *desirable*, that is, what we not only want but feel that it is right and proper to want for ourselves and for others. . . . [Values are] abstract standards that transcend the impulses of the moment and ephemeral situations.[3]

It is the sense of "ought" that distinguishes values from ordinary desires or needs. For instance, truth is something not only desirable but we feel that we ought to be truthful. Values are inner imperatives which urge us to seek higher goals. The distinguished Indian social scientist Radhakamal Mukerjee offers the following clarification:

> The psychological and social sciences dealing with values define them as mere preferences, as desirable goals, emotions, and interests. The humanistic disciplines, on the other hand, define them as functioning imperatives or "oughts."[4]

We have seen that values are higher needs and are also inner imperatives or oughts. They have one more characteristic: they belong to the whole society or community or even the whole humanity. It is not what any individual thinks as desirable that is called value, but what the whole community or majority of people think as desirable. That is to say, values are certain social norms or standards. Values belong to culture. Explaining this, the authors of a popular book on psychology state: "A cultural value may be defined as a widely held belief or sentiment that some activities, relationships, feelings or goals are important to the community's identity or well-being."[5]

Combining all the three characteristics of values, we may now give a comprehensive definition: Values are the higher normative needs of humanity which individuals experience as inner moral or aesthetic imperatives or goal seeking.

Another concept frequently confused with values is the ideal. An ideal is nothing but a *value chosen as the goal of life* by an individual.

Expressions of the Evolutionary Urge

According to some thinkers, values, ¿
inborn desire in man for self-improvement, the ın..
seek higher and higher levels of fulfillment, represent ı.
higher evolutionary urge. Says the eminent biologist Julian
Huxley: "We find values not only emerging from the evolutionary process but playing an active part in its latest phase; we
know as an immediate and obvious fact that there are higher and
lower values, we discover as a result of scientific analysis that
there are more or less desirable and valuable directions in evolution."[6]

Radhakamal Mukerjee adds: "Such a directive quality of
adjustment of organism to the environment at the dimension of
human social evolution is called values which influence the
course of evolution toward greater individuality and openness
of self and purposive direction of self and environment. . . . Ru-
diments of values are discernible among the brainy animals. But
no animal, including the lower primates, can develop a set of
values that direct and regulate behavior around long-term goals
or evolve a symbolic complex helping them to accumulate, reorganize and anticipate experiences."[7]

That is to say, values are not mere individual desires and
fancies but are expressions of the creative power of universal
Life. The river of life is flowing through all, and values mark the
higher points of its rising tide. There is in man an intrinsic urge
to seek higher levels of existence, higher levels of consciousness, and higher levels of happiness. Values are manifestations
of this urge.

It may, however, be mentioned here that this lofty view of
values is no longer in vogue now. The tendency in recent years
is to treat values merely as interests or desires. R. B. Perry, who
is one of the proponents of this view, says: "A thing—anything—has value or is valuable when it is the object of an interest, any interest. Or whatever is an object of interest is *ipso facto*

.aluable."[8] Here interest includes both likes and dislikes.

Types of Values

Values do not belong to one field of experience alone but to different fields. Hence we have several kinds of values. The most well-known of these are moral values, known as virtues, such as truthfulness, kindness, equality, and so on. Apart from these, there are social values, aesthetic values, cognitive values, and spiritual values. Each class of values pertains to a particular dimension of personality. The pursuit of all the five classes of values mentioned above is necessary for the all-round development of personality.

Not all values, however, are of equal importance. Some of the values are regarded as an end in themselves; these are called absolute values. Values which are regarded as a means for the attainment of some higher goal are called instrumental values. Which values are regarded as absolute and which as instrumental depends upon the culture to which the values belong.

The Greek culture from very ancient times regarded Truth, Goodness, and Beauty as absolute values. From the Greeks this concept passed on to the Romans and to later Western culture. Christian religion posited love of God as the absolute value and love for man as an instrumental value. These ideas also passed on to Western culture, but they never became its dominant characteristics.

Indian culture has adopted, right from very ancient times, a two-tier system of values which are known as *puruṣārthas*. The lower tier consists of three values: *kāma* (sensuous pleasure), *artha* (wealth) and *dharma* (morality). Hindu scriptures clearly state that *kāma* and *artha* should be governed by *dharma*. This triad of values is meant for ordinary people. For those who have developed dispassion for the world, Hindu culture offers the upper tier which forms the highest value (*parama puruṣārtha*) namely, *mukti* or *mokṣa*, everlasting freedom. There is hardly anyone who does not want to be free from sorrow. *Mukti*, however, is not freedom from ordinary sorrow but from the very possibility of being reborn on earth. *Mukti* is an absolute value. The lower three values may be regarded as instrumental values, although they do not necessarily lead to *mukti*.

Values and Reality

Though there are similarities between the Indian and Western approaches to value, we have to keep in mind that the whole concept of value is characteristically Western. Plato is believed to have originated the study of values, but it was only toward the end of the 19th century that it was reorganized as an independent discipline under the name of Axiology. Since then several Western philosophers have regarded values as the main object of philosophical enquiry and as the ultimate goal of life. But are values an end in themselves? Can mere pursuit of values be regarded as the ultimate goal of life? Are not values only pointers to an ultimate thing valued?

The last question may be answered first. In the ordinary practical world we find that the word "value" usually refers to something which is valued. For instance, when the shopkeeper tells us that the price of a kilo of potatoes is five rupees, what he means is that a potato is a valuable thing. The five rupees we pay is only a symbol of the abstract idea of its value. The potato is the real thing; it satisfies our hunger. The money we pay, its value, is only a token; it cannot by itself satisfy our hunger.

This is true of higher values also. Values are intangible abstract concepts which have their ultimate source in certain aspects of Reality. Values have no existence apart from the Reality they represent. Values only stimulate the quest for lasting fulfillment, but they cannot by themselves give that fulfillment. They only tantalize like a mirage, and goad people to something beyond them. But lasting fulfillment can come only through the transcendental realization of the ultimate Reality.

insight into the ultimate meaning and purpose of life
was always provided Indian culture its main thrust. From very
ancient times orientation to the ultimate Reality has provided
the basic discipline to the best minds in India. It was assumed
that if Reality orientation was done in the proper way, value orientation would follow in a natural way. Orientation to Reality
had always formed the core subject of the Indian system of education until the beginning of the modern age. And, as the stories
of children in the Upanishads indicate, this orientation to Reality began early in boyhood. In the *Chāndogya Upaniṣad* we find
a boy named Satyakama gains direct knowledge of *Brahman*
through communion with nature, and another boy, Upakosala,
feels depressed because of his teacher's refusal to instruct him
about *Brahman*.

By contrast, value orientation has been the dominant characteristic of Western culture. It is doubtful whether the ancient
Greeks attained direct realization of the ultimate Reality. As discussions in Plato's works indicate, Greek culture was primarily
value-oriented, and this tradition became a heritage for Western
people. Although Christianity produced many illumined saints,
direct mystical experience of the ultimate Reality never became
an essential aspect of Western culture.

Right from Plato's time Western culture has cherished
Beauty, Truth, and Goodness as the ultimate values. Art, science, and social service are regarded as the pursuit of these three
values respectively. In all these three fields the West has many
achievements to its credit. But it has not found the way to lasting
fulfillment and peace, nor has it been able to stem the tide of
degradation. A few years ago the Foundation for Advanced Information and Research, Japan, published a series of reports
based on research conducted by several Study Groups. One of
the reports states: "The affluent society has altered the desires,
behavioral patterns and social structures of its people. These
changes include the formation of a new upper class, the frag-
mentation of values, and the appearance of a pathological social

phenomena, the so-called 'advanced nation's syndrome,' in rich societies. . . . This malaise affects not only the economies of the countries involved, but its symptoms penetrate the political and social spheres as well. As a result, the advanced industrial societies are faced not only with declining economic vitality, but also with a variety of manifestations of anomie, such as decreasing political unity, terrorism, crime, juvenile delinquency, suicide, anxiety and depression, alcoholism, drug addiction, the loss of the will to work, and sexual confusion."

Science and technology have orientated the minds of people in the West also wholly to the physical world, and Western culture has become thoroughly materialistic. In such a situation traditional values have become inoperative resulting in a crisis of values. The basic cause of this crisis is that the Western conception of values is not rooted in a clear perception or understanding of the ultimate Reality.

Here comes the importance of the Vedantic vision of *Brahman*, the ultimate Reality, as *Sat-Cit-Ānanda* (Being-Awareness-Bliss Absolute). This view can provide the reality support that the Western concept of Beauty, Truth, and Goodness as ultimate values very much stands in need of. Beauty, Truth, and Goodness may be regarded as *Sat, Cit* and *Ānanda* perceived through the veil of *māyā*. Vedantic scriptures state that *Brahman* manifests itself in the empirical world as *asti, bhāti,* and *priyam.*[9] These may be said to correspond to Beauty, Truth, and Goodness.

Yoga, the Connecting Link

The main thesis we have been trying to establish is this: Value orientation must be supported by Reality orientation. Values have no value in themselves. It is the Reality behind the values that gives them power. Values must be rooted in Reality.

This principle applies not only at the higher level of philosophical thinking where Beauty, Truth, and Goodness appear as

SWAMI BHAJANANANDA

abstract concepts or ideals, but also at the lower level of practicing the simple virtues of ordinary life. It is not enough to preach to young people about values or virtues; they should be shown how to make the values or virtues real in their lives. It is no use telling a young man, "Be fearless," unless the deep-rooted cause of fear in him is removed. What is the use of talking to a person about the value of love if he has received no love from his parents or other people?

In this context it is worth quoting what Swami Vivekananda said in one of his lectures on *Rāja Yoga*,

> We hear "be good," "be good," and "be good," taught all over the world. There is hardly a child, born in any country in the world, who has not been told, "Do not steal," "Do not tell a lie," but nobody tells the child how he can help doing them. Talking will not help him. . . . Only when we teach him to control his mind do we really help him.[10]

In order to attain value fulfillment we have to confront the reality that it represents. This calls for self-discipline in the form of self-control, self-knowledge, and inward concentration. This kind of self-discipline in due course brings about transformation of one's consciousness which is what Yoga means. On this point Swami Vivekananda says,

> We have to get the power to become moral; until we do that, we cannot control our actions. Yoga alone enables us to carry into practice the teachings of morality. To become moral is the object of Yoga.[11]

Yoga is, thus, the connecting link between values and Reality. Yoga transforms value experience into mystic experience. Yoga gives us the power to go beyond values and realize the Reality which they symbolize. Without Yoga, values remain mere dreams of poets and preachers.

Unfortunately, there is much misunderstanding about Yoga in the East as well as in the West. For many people Yoga means nothing more than some postural exercises. But true Yoga is an inner discipline for the transformation of consciousness through self-knowledge, self-control, and self-directed activity. Though there are special techniques for this transformation such as *jñāna yoga, bhakti yoga, rāja yoga*, and so on, any work, any activity, can be done as Yoga. Education—both teaching and learning—can be done as Yoga. Pursuit of art, science, or social service can be done as Yoga. Indeed, one's whole life can be converted into Yoga. In the *Gītā*, Lord Krishna describes the whole creation as "Divine Yoga."[12] Of course, the Yoga that is spoken of here is only of the preliminary type. But it is nevertheless important. Its importance lies in the fact that it gives to the soul proper Reality orientation.

Two-Level Unfoldment

The transformation of consciousness that Yoga brings about is, from the standpoint of *Advaita Vedanta*, a form of unveiling or unfolding of the inner Self. According to Vedanta, man's real nature is neither the body nor the mind but the Self known as the *Ātman*. This true Self is of the nature of pure, unchanging, self-luminous awareness which is immortal and is the source of all knowledge, all happiness, all power. Furthermore, all individual selves are only reflections of one universal supreme Self. However, owing to beginningless ignorance known as *māyā* or *avidyā*, the inner Self remains veiled. Cognition removes a bit of this ignorance; then the Self manifests itself and its light reveals the object as knowledge. This is how every kind of knowledge takes place. Explaining this process, Swami Vivekananda says,

> Knowledge is inherent in man; no knowledge comes from outside; it is all inside. What we say a man knows, should in strict psychological parlance be what he discovers, by taking the cover off his own soul, which is a mine of infinite knowledge.[13]

In other words, every kind of knowledge—even the lowest

form of sense experience—is the result of the self-manifestation of the *Ātman*.

What, then, is the difference between ordinary empirical knowledge and higher transcendental knowledge? The answer is, although the manifestation of the *Ātman* takes place in both the types of experience, the nature of knowledge is determined by the type of ignorance involved. According to Vedanta, ignorance is of two kinds: empirical ignorance (known as *tūlāvidyā*) and causal ignorance (known as *mūlāvidyā*). The first one is ignorance regarding empirical objects, whereas the second one is ignorance concerning the ultimate Reality, the true nature of the *Ātman*.

In empirical knowledge the removal of only *tūlāvidyā*, empirical ignorance, takes place. This is the fundamental mental process taking place in education. Learning removes only empirical ignorance, but this is enough to give us knowledge of the external world and bring out the talents and capacities inherent in individual minds. This was, perhaps what Swami Vivekandanda meant when he gave the famous definition, "Education is the manifestation of the perfection already in man."

But this kind of empirical knowledge which we gain through education does not remove causal ignorance. Only transcendental knowledge gained through Yoga can remove causal ignorance. When causal ignorance is removed, the *Ātman* reveals or manifests itself in all its glory. This experience known as Self-realization or God-realization is the essential meaning and purpose of Religion. The idea that "Religion is [transcendental] realization" has gained popularity in modern times mainly through the teachings of Sri Ramakrishna and Swami Vivekananda. Swamiji did not, however, want religious experience to be restricted to the transcendental plane alone. He wanted that the higher knowledge should manifest itself through the attitudes and actions of the individual in the world, and should help him to face the problem of social life. Hence

Swamiji gave a new definition of religion: "Religion is the manifestation of the Divinity already in man." Explaining this he stated in another context:

> My ideal, indeed, can be put into a few words, and that is: to preach unto mankind their divinity, and how to make it manifest in every movement of life.[14]

So then, according to Swami Vivekananda, education and religion are two phases of a single process of Self-revelation or Self-realization. Pursuit of values and quest for the ultimate Reality are both manifestations of man's innate evolutionary urge at two planes of existence. Such a view transforms education into a spiritual discipline, removes the distinction between the secular and the sacred, and makes one's life a ceaseless striving for higher degrees of love, knowledge, and happiness. Such a holistic view alone can make life meaningful, harmonious, and peaceful. This is the integral philosophy of life that the world is very much in need of now.

FOOTNOTES:

[1] Abraham Maslow, *The Farther Reaches of Human Nature*, p. 106.
[2] Abraham Maslow, *Motivation and Personality*.
[3] Clyde Kluckhohn, *Culture and Behaviour*, p. 289.
[4] Radhakamal Mukerjee, *The Dimensions of Value*.
[5] Leonard Broom and Philip Selznic, *Principles of Sociology*, p. 54.
[6] Julian Huxley, *Evolution and Ethics*, p. 32.
[7] Radhakamal Mukerjee, *The Dimensions of Value*.
[8] Ralph Barton Perry, *The Realms of Value*.
[9] *Dṛg-Dṛsya-Viveka*, p. 20.
[10] *Complete Works of Swami Vivekananda*, 1:171 (hereafter as cited as CW).
[11] CW.8:43.
[12] *Bhagavad Gītā*, 9:5;11:8.
[13] CW. 1:28.
[14] CW. 7:498.

II

The Three Principles
of Hinduism

by Swami Chinmayananda

To realize our all-full spiritual Nature is to experience the fullness of life. As long as we have not attained this state of being our intellect will continue to suggest methods for overcoming feelings of imperfection, which manifest as desires. Desires are nothing but an expression of the ignorance of our real Nature. This ignorance has made us identify with the body, mind, and intellect, and is the cause of our egocentric life of pains and limitations. Therefore, there is no achievement more sacred and glorious than the realization of our true identity with the unlimited, eternal Self.

The purpose of religion is to eliminate ignorance through spiritual practices until the devotee comes to gain the light of wisdom. Ignorance, manifesting as desires on the mental plane, extend themselves as actions in the world. Therefore, spiritual masters advise that the most practical way of overcoming ignorance is through controlling our actions. They suggest that we first purify, and regulate these actions. All religions advocate qualities such as goodness, kindness, tolerance, mercy, and selflessness. They insist on moral and ethical perfection as the fundamental condition for spiritual evolution. Without these qualities we will end up far short of the goal, even after a lifetime of devotion and worship.

Let us try to understand the scope of these moral and ethical values as explained in Hinduism. The three corner stones upon which the temple of Hinduism has been built are self-control, non-injury, and truthfulness. The vast amount of spiritual literature in India is nothing but annotations, amplifications, and commentaries upon these three principles. Ancient Indians planned their individual, communal, and national life upon these three fundamental duties.

When these values are practiced they enable us to master our mind, which leads to mastery over ourselves and the world around us. Although these principles are essentially the same in all religions, differences may appear due to the way in which they were presented to meet the needs of the people of the time. These three fundamental moral codes of behavior are: self-control (*brahmacarya*), non-injury (*ahiṁsā*), and truthfulness (*satyam*). They are the source of all values, and refer to the three layers of our personality: physical, emotional, and intellectual.

Self-Control

The physical body longs for contact with the world of objects in order to gain sense gratification. The eyes wish to see beautiful forms and colors, the tongue craves good food, the nose likes to smell pleasant fragrances, and so on. But when we continue to live only for the gratification of our sensual demands, passions multiply and ultimately consume us. To avoid such a condition, discipline at the physical level, *brahmacarya*, is prescribed. The meaning of the word *brahmacarya* has been so badly distorted that the real value of this discipline has been lost. *Brahmacarya* is an attitude of intelligent contact with the world. It does not mean a total denial of sense enjoyments, but only insists on not overdoing anything. Thus to read, watch television, talk, or walk too much, or to eat a morsel more than is necessary would be considered as breaking the vow of *brahmacarya*. When we live in self-control we discover in ourselves a renewed dynamism, and become pillars of strength in society. If this sacred doctrine is not followed, we abdicate our own freedom and become slaves to the ever-changing circumstances of life. Thus, *brahmacarya* is a value to be lived at the physical level.

Non-Injury

The second discipline, prescribed for the mental level, is non-injury *(ahiṁsā)*. *Ahiṁsā* does not simply mean non-killing or non-injury at the physical level. It is to be understood as a mental attitude regarding our relationship with others. Non-injury is the spirit that should dominate the realm of our motives. Sometimes it is necessary that our actions be cruel although the underlying motive is totally loving and kind. Shakespeare beautifully expressed this idea in Hamlet, "I am cruel only to be kind." For example, a surgeon may outwardly appear to be cruel while performing an operation but his motive is honorable. Such actions, though causing physical pain, would be considered as *ahiṁsā*. To physically resist a burglar in our homes or standing up to unwise policies of a priest or politician, is not transgressing *ahiṁsā*. Non-injury is not a passive ineffectual attitude. Restraining the wicked to protect the good is the very creed of every true Hindu.

Thus, non-injury, as advised by the architects of the Hindu culture, is a value of life to be applied at the level of our motives. Our motives should be blessed and pure without any cruelty or hatred. In the execution of a pure motive, we may have to weed out the thorny shrubs to make the garden beautiful again.

Truthfulness

Satyam or truthfulness is the means to govern our inner world of mind and intellect. The outer world is a great university providing us with innumerable opportunities from which to learn. When these experiences have been well churned in our mind and the intellect has come to a firm decision, we must have the honesty and conviction to act upon it. When we do not make full use of our mind and intellect they lose their efficiency and we suffer as a result. Religion constantly reminds us to exercise our mind and intellect through its insistence upon the principle, "Be truthful to your previously gained wisdom."

Thus, truthfulness enjoins us to live according to our intellectual convictions. We all have ideals, but we often fall prey to our senses and compromise with them. This is dishonest living. Our dignity depends on our ability to live up to our convictions at all times.

The edifice of life stands on these three great principles. By following them we can integrate our personality and gain inner health. It is by this method alone that we can enjoy living in the world and develop the strength and courage to overcome all our problems in life.

When a person has learned to live in perfect self-control, ever vigilant to gather knowledge from life's experiences, practicing non-injury in his motives, and being truthful to his convictions, he becomes the chosen child of nature to be lifted to the top of the evolutionary ladder.

It is true, no doubt, that there are only a few in society who practice these great principles, but those few grow to such a stature that they lead the world with an irresistible spiritual power. It is these people of heroic personality, with integrated head and heart, who will continue to guide humanity to new levels of spiritual evolution.

III

Expanding Our Spiritual Practice

by Jack Kornfield

We must remember that the world's current problems are fundamentally a spiritual crisis, created by the limited vision of human beings—a loss of a sense of connection to one another, a loss of community, and most deeply a loss of connection to our spiritual values.

Political and economic change have never been sufficient in themselves to alleviate suffering when the underlying causes are not also addressed. The worst problems on this earth—warfare, poverty, ecological destruction, and so forth—are created from greed, hatred, prejudice, delusion, and fear in the human mind. To expand the circle of our practice and to face the sorrow in the world around us, we must face these forces in ourselves. Einstein called us nuclear giants and ethical infants. Only when we have found a compassion, a goodness and understanding, that transcends our own greed, hatred, and delusion, can we bring freedom alive in the world around us.

A wide and open heart gives us the strength to face the world directly, to understand the roots of our sorrows and our part in them. President Dwight Eisenhower reminded us of this responsibility when he stated:

> Every gun that is made, every warship launched, every rocket fired signifies, in the final sense, a theft from those who are

cold and not clothed. This world in arms is not spending money alone. It is spending the sweat of its laborers, the genius of its scientists, the hopes of its children. This is not a way of life at all in its true sense . . . it is humanity hanging from a cross of iron.

It is *our* society that does this. Each of us in a modern society must acknowledge our part in the world dilemma. There are many important levels from which we can address global suffering. We must do what we can in every arena, bringing compassion and skill to economics, to education, to government, to service, and to world conflict. Underlying all this work we must find a strength of heart to face injustice with truth and compassion.

There are two sources of strength in our world. One is the force of hatred, of those who are unafraid to kill. The other and greater strength comes from those who are unafraid to die. This was the strength behind Gandhi's marches against the entire British Empire, the strength of Dorothy Day's tireless work for the poor on the streets of New York. This strength of heart and being is that which has reclaimed and redeemed human life in every circumstance.

Awakening compassion and freedom on this earth will not be easy. We need to be honest in dishonest times, when it is easier to fight for our principles than to live up to them. We must awaken in a time when the Tao, the *dharma*, the universal laws are often forgotten, when materialism, possessiveness, indulgence, and military security are widely advertised as the correct basis for human action. These ways are not the *dharma*, they do not follow timeless laws of human harmony and human happiness. This we can see for ourselves. We must find or discover in ourselves the ancient and eternal law of life based on truth and compassion to guide our actions.

Conscious Conduct

To widen our understanding and compassion, our action

must be in harmony with these ancient laws of conscious conduct. These laws alone are the basis of conscious spiritual life, and to follow and refine them in every circumstance is itself a practice leading to liberation of all beings.

I saw one of the clearest examples of these laws demonstrated in the Cambodian refugee camps. I was with a friend and teacher, Mahaghosananda, an extraordinary Cambodian monk, one of the few to survive, when he opened a Buddhist temple in a barren refugee camp of the Khmer Rouge communists. There were fifty thousand villagers who had become communists at gunpoint and had now fled the destruction to camps on the Thai border. In this camp the underground Khmer Rouge camp leaders threatened to kill any who would go to the temple. Yet on its opening day more than twenty thousand people crowded into the dusty square for the ceremony. These were the sad remnants of families, an uncle with two nieces, a mother with only one of three children. The schools had been burned, the villages destroyed, and in nearly every family, members had been killed or ripped away. I wondered what he would say to people who had suffered so greatly.

Mahaghosananda began the service with the traditional chants that had permeated village life for a thousand years. Though these words had been silenced for eight years and the temples destroyed, they still remained in the hearts of these people whose lives had known as much sorrow and injustice as any on earth. Then Mahaghosananda began chanting one of the central verses of the Buddha, first in Pali and then in Cambodian, reciting the words over and over.

> Hatred never ceases by hatred
> but by love alone is healed.
> This is an ancient and eternal law.

As he chanted these verses over and over thousands chanted with him. They chanted and wept. It was an amazing moment, for it was clear that the truth he chanted was even greater than their sorrows.

Every great spiritual tradition recognizes and teaches the basic laws of wise and conscious human conduct. Whether called virtues, ethics, moral conduct, or precepts, they are guidelines for living without bringing harm to others; they bring sanity and light into the world. In every human being, there is the capacity to take joy in virtue, in integrity, and in uprightness of heart. When we care for one another and live without harming other beings, we create freedom and happiness.

IV

The Five Precepts
of Buddhism

by Thich Nhat Hanh

Precepts in Buddhism and commandments in Judaism and Christianity are important jewels that we need to study and practice. They provide guidelines that can help us transform our suffering. Looking deeply at these precepts and commandments, we can learn the art of living in beauty. The Five Wonderful Precepts of Buddhism—reverence for life, generosity, responsible sexual behavior, speaking and listening deeply, and ingesting only wholesome substances—can contribute greatly to the happiness of the family and society. I have recently rephrased them to address the problems of our times:

Reverence for Life

> *1. Aware of the suffering caused by the destruction of life, I vow to cultivate compassion and learn ways to protect the lives of people, animals, plants, and minerals. I am determined not to kill, not to let others kill, and not to condone any act of killing in the world, in my thinking and in my way of life.*

The First Precept is born from the awareness that lives everywhere are being destroyed. We see the suffering caused by the destruction of life, and we vow to cultivate compassion and use it as a source of energy for the protection of people, animals, plants, and minerals. No act of killing can be justified. And not to kill is not enough. We must also learn ways to prevent others from killing. We cannot condone any act of killing, even in our minds. According to the Buddha, the mind is the base of all actions. When you believe, for example, that yours is the only way for humankind, millions of people might be killed because of that idea. We have to look deeply every day to practice this precept well. Every time we buy or consume something, we may be condoning some form of killing.

To practice nonviolence, first of all we must learn to deal peacefully with ourselves. In us, there is a certain amount of violence and a certain amount of nonviolence. Depending on the state of our being, our response to things will be more or less nonviolent. With mindfulness—the practice of peace—we can begin by working to transform the wars in ourselves. Conscious breathing helps us do this. But no one can practice this precept perfectly. We should not be too proud about being a vegetarian, for example. We must acknowledge that the water in which we boil our vegetables contains many tiny microorganisms, not to mention the vegetables themselves. But even if we cannot be completely nonviolent, by being vegetarian we are going in the direction of nonviolence. If we want to head north, we can use the North Star to guide us, but it is impossible to arrive at the North Star. Our effort is only to proceed in that direction. If we create true harmony within ourselves, we will know how to deal with family, friends, and society.

Life is so precious, yet in our daily lives we are usually carried away by our forgetfulness, anger, and worries. The practice of the First Precept is a celebration of reverence for life. When we appreciate and honor the beauty of life, we will make every effort to dwell deeply in the present moment and protect all life.

Generosity

   2. Aware of the suffering caused by exploitation, social injustice, stealing, and oppression, I vow to cultivate loving-

*kindness and learn ways to work for the well-being of people,
animals, plants, and minerals. I vow to practice generosity by
sharing my time, energy, and material resources with those
who are in real need. I am determined not to steal and not to
possess anything that should belong to others. I will respect
the property of others, but I will prevent others from profiting
from human suffering or the suffering of other species on
Earth.*

The Five Precepts inter-are. When you practice one Precept
deeply, you practice all five. The First Precept is about taking
life which is a form of stealing. When we meditate on the Second
Precept, we see that stealing, in the forms of exploitation,
social injustice, and oppression, is an act of killing.

Instead of stealing, we practice generosity. In Buddhism,
we say there are three kinds of gifts: (1) the gift of material
resources, (2) the gift of helping people rely on themselves, and
(3) the gift of nonfear. But it takes time to practice generosity.
Sometimes one pill or a little rice could save the life of a child,
but we do not think we have the time to help. The best use of
our time is being generous and really being present with others.
People of our time tend to overwork, even when they are not in
great need of money. We seem to take refuge in our work in
order to avoid confronting our real sorrow and inner turmoil.
We express our love and care for others by working hard, but if
we do not have time for the people we love, if we cannot make
ourselves available to them, how can we say that we love them?

True love needs mindfulness. We have to take the time to
acknowledge the presence of the person we love. "Darling, I
know you are there, and I am happy." This cannot be done if we
cannot free ourselves from our preoccupations and our forgetfulness. In order to acknowledge the presence of our beloved
one, we have to offer our own true presence. Without the practice of establishing ourselves in the here and the now, this seems
impossible. Mindful time spent with the person we love is the
fullest expression of true love and real generosity. One twelve-
year-old boy, when asked by his father what he would like for

his birthday, said, "Daddy, I want you!" His father was rarely at home. He was quite wealthy, but he worked all the time to provide for his family. His son was a "bell of mindfulness" for him. The little boy understood that the greatest gift we can offer our loved ones is our true presence.

Responsible Sexual Behavior

> *3. Aware of the suffering caused by sexual misconduct, I vow to cultivate responsibility and learn ways to protect the safety and integrity of individuals, couples, families, and society. I am determined not to engage in sexual relations without love and a long-term commitment. To preserve the happiness of myself and others, I am determined to respect my commitments and the commitments of others. I will do everything in my power to protect children from sexual abuse and to prevent couples and families from being broken by sexual misconduct.*

So many individuals, children, couples, and families have been destroyed by sexual misconduct. To practice the Third Precept is to heal ourselves and heal our society. This is mindful living.

The feeling of loneliness is universal. We believe in a naive way that having a sexual relationship will make us feel less lonely. But without communication on the level of the heart and spirit, a sexual relationship will only widen the gap and harm us both. We know that violating this precept causes severe problems, but still we do not practice it seriously. Couples engage in infidelity; and jealousy, anger, and despair are the result. When the children grow up, they repeat the same mistakes, yet the violation of this precept continues to be encouraged in magazines, TV shows, films, books, and so on. We constantly encounter themes that arouse sexual desire, often coupled with themes of violence. If our collective consciousness is filled with violent sexual seeds, why should we be surprised when there is sexual abuse of children, rape, and other violent acts?

In the Buddhist tradition, we speak of the oneness of body and mind. Whatever happens to the body also happens to the mind. The sanity of the body is the sanity of the mind; the violation of the body is the violation of the mind. A sexual relationship is an act of communion between body and spirit. This is a very important encounter, not to be done in a casual manner. In our soul there are certain areas—memories, pain, secrets—that are private, that we would share only with the person we love and trust the most. We do not open our heart and show it to just anyone.

The same is true of our body. Our bodies have areas that we do not want anyone to touch or approach unless he or she is the one we respect, trust, and love the most. When we are approached casually or carelessly, with an attitude that is less than tender, we feel insulted in our body and soul. Someone who approaches us with respect, tenderness, and utmost care is offering us deep communication, deep communion. It is only in that case that we will not feel hurt, misused, or abused, even a little. This cannot be attained unless there is true love and commitment. Casual sex cannot be described as love. Love is deep, beautiful, and whole, integrating body and spirit.

True love contains respect. In my tradition, husband and wife are expected to respect each other like guests, and when you practice this kind of respect, your love and happiness will continue for a long time. In sexual relationships, respect is one of the most important elements. Sexual communion should be like a rite, a ritual performed in mindfulness with great respect, care, and love. Mere desire is not love. Without the communion of souls, the coming together of the two bodies can create division, widening the gap and causing much suffering.

Love is much more responsible. It has care in it and it involves the willingness and capacity to understand and to make the other person happy. In true love, happiness is not an individual matter. If the other person is not happy, it will be impossible for us to be happy ourselves. True happiness is not possible without a certain degree of calmness and peace in our heart and in our body. Passion or excitement contains within it the element of disturbance. True love is a process of learning and practice that brings in more elements of peace, harmony, and happiness. The phrase "long-term commitment" does not express the depth of love we feel for our partner, but we have to say something so people understand. A long-term commitment is only a beginning. We also need the support of friends and other people. That is why we have a wedding ceremony. Two families join together with other friends to witness the fact that the couple has come together to live. The priest and the marriage license are just symbols. What is important is that the commitment is witnessed by friends and both of the families. "Responsibility" is the key word. The Third Precept should be practiced by everyone. . . .

Speaking and Listening Deeply

> *4. Aware of the suffering caused by unmindful speech and the inability to listen to others, I vow to cultivate loving speech and deep listening in order to bring joy and happiness to others and relieve others of their suffering. Knowing that words can create happiness or suffering, I vow to learn to speak truthfully, with words that inspire self-confidence, joy, and hope. I am determined not to spread news that I do not know to be certain and not to criticize or condemn things of which I am not sure. I will refrain from uttering words that can cause division or discord, or that can cause the family or the community to break. I will make all efforts to reconcile and resolve all conflicts, however small.*

In the Buddhist tradition, the Fourth Precept is described as refraining from these four actions: (1) Not telling the truth. If it's black, you say it's white. (2) Exaggerating. You make something up, or describe something as more beautiful than it actually is, or as ugly when it is not so ugly. (3) Forked tongue. You go to one person and say one thing and then you go to another person and say the opposite. (4) Filthy language. You insult or abuse people.

This precept admonishes us not to lie, not to say things that destroy friendships and relationships, but to use wholesome, loving speech. It is as important as the Third Precept in preventing families from being broken. Speaking unmindfully or irresponsibly can destroy us, because when we lie, we lose faith in our own beauty and we lose the trust of others. We have to dissolve all prejudices, barriers, and walls and empty ourselves in order to listen and look deeply before we utter even one word. When we are mindful of our words, it helps us, our families, and our society. We also need to practice the Fourth Precept as individuals and as a nation. We have to work to undo the misunderstandings that exist between the United States and Vietnam, France and Germany, Norway and Sweden, and so on. And we must not underestimate the misunderstandings between religious traditions. Church leaders, diplomats, and all of us need to practice this precept carefully.

Never in the history of humankind have we had so many means of communication, yet we remain islands. There is little real communication between the members of one family, between the individuals in society, and between nations. We have not cultivated the arts of listening and speaking. We have to learn ways to communicate again. When we cannot communicate, we get sick, and as our sickness worsens, our suffering spills onto other people. When it has become too difficult to share and to communicate with those in our family, we want to go to a psychotherapist, hoping that he or she will listen to our suffering. Psychotherapists are also human beings. There are those who can listen deeply to us and those who, because they themselves have suffered so much, do not have the capacity. Psychotherapists have to train themselves in the art of listening with calm and compassion. How can someone who has so much suffering within himself or herself, so much anger, irritation, fear, and despair, listen deeply to us? If you wish to see a psychotherapist, try to find someone who is happy and who can communicate well with his or her spouse, children, friends, and society.

Training ourselves in the art of mindful breathing is crucial for knowing how to take care of our emotions. First, we recognize the presence of, for example, anger in us, and we allow it to be. We do not try to suppress it or express it. We just bring the energy of mindfulness to our anger and allow our mindfulness to take care of it the way a mother holds her baby when it begins to cry. We do this by practicing mindful breathing, while sitting or while walking. Walking alone in a park or along a river, coordinating our steps with our breath, is a very effective way to care for our anger, to calm it down.

In his Discourse on Mindful Breathing, the Buddha taught, "Breathing in, I recognize my feeling. Breathing out, I calm my feeling." If you practice this, not only will your feeling be calmed down but the energy of mindfulness will also help you see into the nature and roots of your anger. Mindfulness helps you be concentrated and look deeply. This is true meditation. The insight will come after some time of practice. You will see the truth about yourself and the truth about the person who you thought to be the cause of your suffering. This insight will release you from your anger and transform the roots of anger in you. The transformation in you will also help transform the other person.

Mindful speaking can bring real happiness, and unmindful speech can kill. When someone tells us something that makes us happy, that is a wonderful gift. But sometimes someone says something to us that is so cruel and distressing that we feel like committing suicide. We lose our *joie de vivre*.

The Fourth Precept is also linked to the Second Precept, on stealing. Many people have to lie in order to succeed as politicians or salespersons. A corporate director of communications told me that if he were allowed to tell the truth about his company's products, people would not buy them. He says positive things about the products that he knows are not true, and he refrains from speaking about their negative effects. He knows he is lying, and he feels terrible about it. Many people are caught in this kind of situation. In politics, people lie to get votes.

This precept is also linked with the Third Precept, on sexual responsibility. When someone says, "I love you," it may be a lie. It may just be an expression of desire. So much advertising is linked with sex. There is a saying in Vietnamese: "It doesn't cost anything to have loving speech." We only need to choose our words carefully, and we can make other people happy. To use words mindfully, with loving kindness, is to practice generosity. Therefore this precept is linked directly to the Second Precept. We can make many people happy just by practicing loving speech. Again, we see the interbeing nature of the Five Precepts.

Ingesting Wholesome Substances

> 5. Aware of the suffering caused by unmindful consumption, I vow to cultivate good health, both physical and mental, for myself, my family, and my society by practicing mindful eating, drinking, and consuming. I vow to ingest only items that preserve peace, well-being, and joy in my body, in my consciousness, and in the collective body and consciousness of my family and society. I am determined not to use alcohol or any other intoxicant or to ingest foods or other items that contain toxins, such as certain TV programs, magazines, books, films, and conversations. I am aware that to damage my body or my consciousness with these poisons is to betray my ancestors, my parents, my society, and future generations. I will work to transform violence, fear, anger, and confusion in myself and in society by practicing a diet for myself and for society. I understand that a proper diet is crucial for self-transformation and for the transformation of society.

In modern life, people think that their body belongs to them and they can do anything they want to it. When they make such a determination, the law supports them. This is one of the manifestations of individualism. But, according to the teachings of emptiness, nonself, and interbeing, your body is not yours alone. It also belongs to your ancestors, your parents, future generations, and all other living beings. Everything, even the trees and the clouds, has come together to bring about the presence of your body. Keeping your body healthy is the best way to express your gratitude to the whole cosmos, to all ancestors, and also not to betray future generations. You practice this precept for everyone. If you are healthy, everyone can benefit from it. When you are able to get out of the shell of your small self, you will see that you are interrelated to everyone and everything, that your every act is linked with the whole of humankind and the whole cosmos. To keep yourself healthy in body and mind is to be kind to all beings. The Fifth Precept is about health and healing.

This precept tells us not to ingest poisons that can destroy our minds and bodies. We should especially avoid alcohol and other intoxicants that cause so much suffering to the individuals involved and to the victims of intoxication—abused family members, those injured in automobile accidents, and so on. Alcohol abuse is one of the main symptoms of the malaise of our times. We know that those who are addicted to alcohol need to abstain one hundred percent. But the Buddha also asked those who have only one glass of wine a week also to refrain from drinking. Why? Because we practice for everyone, including those who have a propensity toward alcoholism. If we give up our glass of wine, it is to show our children, our friends, and our society that our life is not for ourselves alone, but for our ancestors, future generations, and our society also. To stop drinking one glass of wine a week, even if it has not brought us any harm, is a deep practice, the insight of someone who knows that everything we do is for our ancestors and all future generations. I think that the use of drugs by so many young people could be stopped with this kind of insight.

When someone offers you a glass of wine, you can smile and decline, saying, "No thank you. I do not drink alcohol. I would be grateful if you would bring me a glass of juice or water." If you do it gently, with a smile, your refusal is very helpful. It sets an example for many friends, including the children who are present. There are so many delicious and healthy beverages available—why must we continue to honor a beverage that brings about so much suffering? I have asked rabbis, priests, and nuns if they think it would be possible to substitute grape juice for wine in Sabbath rituals, the Eucharist, and other sacramental occasions, and they have said yes.

We must also be careful to avoid ingesting toxins in the form of violent TV programs, video games, movies, magazines, and books. When we watch that kind of violence, we water our own negative seeds, or tendencies, and eventually we will think and act out of those seeds. Because of the violent toxins in so many people's minds, and in our minds, too, it has become dangerous to walk alone at night in many cities. Young people stare at television sets hour after hour, and their minds are invaded by programs selected by irresponsible producers.

The Fifth Precept urges us to find wholesome, spiritual nourishment not only for ourselves but also for our children and future generations. Wholesome, spiritual nourishment can be found by looking at the blue sky, the spring blossoms, or the eyes of a child. The most basic meditation practice of becoming aware of our bodies, our minds, and our world can lead us into a far more rich and fulfilling state than drugs ever could. We can celebrate the joys that are available in these simple pleasures.

The use of alcohol and drugs is causing so much damage to our societies and families. Governments use airplanes, guns, and armies to try to stop the flow of drugs, with little success. Drug users know how destructive their habit is, but they cannot stop. There is so much pain and loneliness inside them, and the use of alcohol and drugs helps them to forget for a while. Once people are addicted to alcohol or drugs, they might do anything to get the drugs they need—lie, steal, rob, or even kill. Trying to stop the drug traffic is not the best use of our resources. Offering education, wholesome alternatives, and hope, and encouraging people to practice the Fifth Precept are much better solutions. To restore our balance and transform the pain and loneliness that are already in us, we have to study and practice the art of touching and ingesting the refreshing, nourishing, and healing elements that are already available. We have to practice together as a family, a community, and a nation. The practice of mindful consuming should become part of our national health policy. Making it so should be a top priority.

The Five Wonderful Precepts are the right medicine to heal us. We need only to observe ourselves and those around us to see the truth. Our stability and the stability of our families and society cannot be obtained without the practice of these precepts. If you look at individuals and families who are unstable and unhappy, you will be astonished to see how many of them do not practice these healthy and life-affirming precepts. You can make the diagnosis yourself and then know that the medicine is available. Practicing these precepts is the best way to restore stability in our families and our society.

The practice of mindfulness is to be aware of what is going on. Once we are able to see deeply the suffering and the roots of the suffering, we will be motivated to act, to practice. The energy we need is not fear or anger, but understanding and compassion. There is no need to blame or condemn. Those who destroy themselves, their families, and their society are not doing it intentionally. Their pain and loneliness are overwhelming, and they want to escape. They need to be helped, not punished. Only understanding and compassion on a collective level can liberate us. The practice of the Five Wonderful Precepts is the practice of mindfulness and compassion. I urge you to practice them as they are presented here, or go back to your own tradition and shed light on the jewels that are already there.

PART TWO

Moral Refinement

*The most important human endeavor is the
striving for morality in our actions.
Our inner balance, and even our very existence
depends on it. Only morality in our actions
can give beauty and dignity to our lives.*

Albert Einstein

Until the mind is purified by the practice of virtue no clear understanding or insight can develop there. It is the consensus of Vedantic teachers that virtue brightens intellect, whereas vice darkens it. An immoral man with all his intelligence can be no better than a clever animal. Being deluded by such vices as greed, lust, pride, hatred, anger, fear, jealousy, he cannot distinguish between the pleasant and the beneficial, between the apparent and the real.

In a fit of anger he may commit a heinous deed and reap the consequences all his life. With his mind distorted by passions and prejudices a man cannot use for his own good what power, knowledge, or riches he has. He will abuse his technical and scientific knowledge as well. With the purification of the mind, knowledge turns into wisdom. Therefore by all means one should overcome vices by the cultivation of virtues.

Swami Satprakashananda
The Goal and the Way

V

Ethics, Morality, and Values

by Swami Chinmayananda

Question: Swamiji, how would you define the words "ethics" and "morality?"

Answer: The word "ethics" is used in a subjective sense, while "morality" is used in relation to the discipline of one's behavior in the world. The right and healthy values of life that we maintain in ourselves comprise ethics, while morality manifests in our behavior concerning the outer world. There are either ethical or unethical thoughts, but immoral thoughts are not possible. There can be moral or immoral action, but there is no such thing as ethical action.

Therefore, one speaks of ethical values and moral behavior. Unless we develop ethical values we cannot live a moral life. Ethics is something we have to cultivate in ourselves, and its expression in the world becomes morality. An ethically bad person cannot be morally good. A moral person acts from the ethical values that he has cultivated in himself.

Q: Is there any relation between ethical norms and religious beliefs?

A: Religion cannot exist without ethical norms and ethics has value only with reference to religion. All ethical principles spring from religion, irrespective of one's beliefs.

Religion explains that moral values are not possible without

God. It is with reference to the Supreme alone that we say something is ultimately good or bad. The standard of comparison by which we can judge anything is God, the Supreme. That is why absolute Goodness, Kindness, Mercy, and Power are all concepts of God.

Looked at from another angle, religion means going beyond one's limited ego in dedication to a higher goal. Only when one aspires to a higher ideal will one be able to withstand the temptations of lower urges. Whenever we act from an egocentric standpoint our actions become immoral. To be moral is to rise above the ego and we all experience this from time to time. For instance, when we become intensely involved in our work or while enjoying the beauty of nature we temporarily lose our sense of individuality.

The Criteria of Judging an Action

Q: Is there any other way that we can judge if an action is good or bad?

A: A reaction in the form of agitation, disturbance, self-criticism, or an accusation shows that an action was wrong. Actions which bring peace, contentment, or self-congratulations to the mind are good actions. Therefore a morally good or bad act depends upon whether the action gives us regret or joy.

Q: Psychoanalysts tell us that we do not take enough notice of our unconscious. To what extent should we trust our instincts?

A: First we need to train our unconscious to function better, only then can we depend on our instincts. If we live according to our present instincts, which are the whisperings of our selfish ego, we are bound to get into trouble. In order to purify our inner instincts we follow moral rules and ethical principles, and live those values uncompromisingly. When we have practiced living the higher values of life for a long period of time, that is, when we have trained our unconscious, then we can depend on our inner voice. When we have become sensitive enough, whatever we do will be morally correct.

Moral Sensitivity

Q: You say that we have to be trained and that it is through experience that we become morally sensitive?

A: Yes, at any moment we act upon that which is morally right for us. It depends upon the grossness or sensitivity of our mind. Everyone comes under the influence of three different moods of the mind, referred to as *guṇas* in Vedanta. These are *Sattva*—purity: thoughts that are pure and noble; *Rajas*—passion: thoughts that are passionate and agitated; and *Tamas*—inertia: thoughts that are dull and inactive. All these three moods are present in us to varying degrees.

Under the influence of *sattva* the mind is calm, creative, inspired, and capable of deep understanding and right choice. Under the influence of *rajas*, the mind is wrought with painful passions, consisting of desires for things not yet acquired, and an attachment to those things already possessed. There will also be a strong egocentric sense that "I am the doer." Under the influence of *tamas*, our intellectual capacity to discriminate between right and wrong becomes veiled. We then live in indolence without any goal or purpose, our thoughts will be dull, and there will be no tenderness of emotion or nobility in action.

If we are mainly *tāmasic* or *rājasic* we will not be sensitive enough to feel the result of our actions. But when we become more *sāttvic* we are more sensitive to disharmony in ourselves and the world. Our capacity to analyze and understand increases, our thoughts will be brilliant, and our actions will be noble.

Q: Thus the intellect judges not only according to the experiences acquired, wisdom gained, but also depending on the mood of the mind at the time of judgment.

A: Yes. The intellect depends on the experiences of the past, but if the mind is disturbed, our judgment and interpretation of the data will be confused. Only later we may realize that a mistake was made. That is why we say that a sin is only wrong judgment, but the judgment was wrong because of the mood of the mind. Had the mind been quieter (more *sāttvic*) then we would not have made a mistake.

Living in Service

Q: How can we become more *sāttvic* and how does that relate to our ultimate goal?

A: Dedicated work is a means for purifying our *vāsanās* (inherent tendencies), thus helping us to become more *sāttvic*. Though the final goal is Self-realization, which is achieved through the path of renunciation, stages of progress from "animal-man" to "God-man" are through an intermediate stage called "man-man."

The Upanishads glorify service as the highest pinnacle to right living. Dedicated and noble work alone can polish us to a state of true culture and right discipline. To those who know what service is, work is not slavery or drudgery, but it is the joy of life. We are not born to revel in idleness.

Vedanta has never allowed escapism, although many uninformed people contend that it does. The earliest Upanishads emphasize that when we cannot live the noble life of renunciation and self-restraint then we must strive to fulfil our desires through honest means. Learning to live in the service of humanity is necessary to prepare us for the highest flights in meditation. Hearing Vedantic discourses may give the listeners a vague concept of the teachings, but only by living as Vedantins can they reach the state of perfection. Vedanta is not divorced from life. In fact, there is no known method of living a fuller life than by organizing it upon a firm foundation of the Vedantic values of Oneness and Truth.

Actions do not cling to one who intensively plunges into

life, eager to meet all its challenges, keeping truth and purity as one's standards at every turn. Such a person lives in the spirit of paying homage to the Lord, detached from the ego-sense and from anxiety for the result of actions. When all activities, whether social, economic, political, or domestic, are pursued in an attitude of detachment, they can never bind anyone by their results.

The highest prayer in the world is service, the greatest devotion is loving the people around, and the noblest character trait is divine compassion for all living creatures.

VI

Stretching Beyond Comfort Zones

by John Powell

It has been said that all of us live in a comfort zone. Try to imagine a circle, big or small, that represents a comfort zone. Then put a dot inside the circle. The dot is you or I and the circle is our comfort zone. We can move around inside the circle and feel comfortable there, but if we move out of the circle, we suffer a panic attack. We are insecure outside that area and feel threatened.

Comfort zones encompass the way we dress and our personal appearance in general. They determine what we can and cannot do. They have a strong effect on the way we deal with people and so forth. A "neatnik" like Felix Unger in *The Odd Couple* would feel uncomfortable in slovenly dress, but roommate Oscar Madison's shoes would immediately become uncomfortable if he shined them. In describing the circumference of our comfort zones, some of us say, for example, "Oh, I just can't give a speech in public," or, "The thought of walking into a roomful of strangers terrifies me," or, "Maybe someone else can do it, but that's just not me."

Sometime make a list of things you just "cannot do." It will give you some idea of the size of your comfort zone. I was surprised by some of those on my list.

The problem is that we huddle carefully inside that comfort

zone; and if it is small, then we are imprisoned in a small world. However, most of us would rather stay in our prisons than pay the price of discomfort for venturing out. We allow ourselves to be painted into a small corner of life. We never find out the limits of our abilities because we never explore them. We don't enjoy our full capacities because we never really test them. It has been said that the average person uses only ten percent of his or her abilities. The other ninety percent gets buried in graves of fear. We fear failure. We fear making a fool out of ourselves. We fear the ridicule of others. We fear criticism. So we cave in and settle down in our comfort corner, and every day begins to look pretty much like yesterday and tomorrow. We wear the same clothes, say the same things, meet the same people, go through the same routines because that is where we are comfortable.

At first it sounds a bit shocking to say, "We must try to overcome all our inhibitions." Sometimes inhibitions are construed as fortunate fences that keep us bound in on the "straight and narrow" paths of virtue. But there is no virtue in inhibition, simply because there is no freedom. For example, I might say something like: "Oh, I just could never tell a lie. I'm sure my cheeks would flush and my nose would grow." I am inhibited. I am held back from lying by the fear that I would not be a successful liar. If this is the case, there is no virtue in my telling the truth. I couldn't do otherwise. Virtue presumes and requires freedom. "I could lie to you, but I choose not to. I want to be a truthful person." This would be an expression of true virtue.

Of course, we don't want to overcome our inhibition to lie by lying. That would really be not letting the left hand know what the right hand is doing. But there are other inhibitions that keep us from freedom and virtue, and these should be directly assaulted by what we call "stretching." For example, a person might say, "I just can't tell those I love that I do love them. So I try to do things for them, to give them gifts. But the words 'I love you' just stick in my throat." The course and the challenge to stretch are clear, "DO IT AND DO IT NOW!" In the consistent practice of this attack on such crippling inhibitions, one eventually becomes a much freer person. And soon he or she will be doing things because "I want to and not because I just couldn't do otherwise." This is a fully human and fully alive person. This is a truly liberated and virtuous person.

Mind and Will

"To stretch," as we use the term here, means "to step outside our comfort zones." It means to dream the impossible dream, to reach for the previously unreached, to try the untried, to risk the possibility of failure, to dare to go into places where we have never been. Obviously, one has to understand clearly the meaning and the advantages of stretching. This is especially true in the beginning, because stretching requires a strong act of the mind and will. I have often imagined our emotions as children surrounding their parents. Mother Mind and Father Will. Often children try to walk tightrope on high fences, to peek over cliffs, and to pet grizzly bears. They kick and cry and squeal when they are not allowed to start dangerous bonfires or throw sharp knives. Mother Mind and Father Will have to be strong and determined. Some parents have insisted that insanity is, in fact, inherited: You get it from your children.

When a person first attempts this challenge of stretching, of stepping out of old comfort zones and into new areas, the children (the emotions) will certainly act up. They will start kicking and screeching, crying and protesting. The imagination (an interior sense) will paint ugly pictures of embarrassment and failure. It will make frightening sounds. "The world will end with a big bang! At least there will be a big explosion. Someone, probably me, will definitely faint. Murphy's Law (What can go wrong will go wrong!) will once more prevail."

But if Mother Mind and Father Will are strong enough, they will prevail. And believe it or not, the world won't go up in smoke. There will be no explosion. No one will faint or die. And old Murphy won't even show up. But that's only some of the things that won't happen. What will result from our stretching is that the world will be widened for us, and our lives will become fuller and more satisfying. Talents will be revealed that we didn't even know we had. Do you remember the first time you swam without someone holding you afloat or the first time you hit a home run? "I can do it!" you announced to yourself and to the world. You didn't drown and you didn't strike out. You did it! A new self-confidence and a new world were created for you in that moment, it always happens when we stretch.

VII

Contentment

by Swami Sivananda

Once a buffalo got disgusted with the hard work of ploughing its master's fields the whole day long. One night, while it was let loose for grazing it ran off to a distant place. It was noticed by a farmer who, knowing that it had strayed away from its owner, made himself its new owner. He yoked it to the plough and made it work day and night.

The buffalo thought: "Oh, what a blunder I have committed by running away from my previous master! He was indeed kind, for he never made me work during the night, but my present master, cruel by nature, makes me work day and night and beats me mercilessly with his whip. I wish I had not deserted my previous master."

The buffalo realized a wonderful truth in life: that no one can escape playing his ordained role in the scheme of God. Any attempt to escape would prove futile and only land one into greater difficulties and forced fulfillment of the assigned role. The buffalo now learned that wisdom lay in meekly surrendering to the Divine Will and discharging one's allotted function, putting up with all the difficulties and inconveniences that one's duty involved.

True Discipline

One cannot expect ideal conditions to prevail anywhere, as

the moment one gets such ideal conditions, the mind will still find some defects in them and crave for still better conditions. It is a trick of the mind to escape discipline. A person of discipline puts up with all conditions, adjusts himself to all situations, and discharges whatever duties are allotted to him. Though it may be difficult, he discharges such duties with a happy and cheerful heart. Such a disciplined person is a true and sincere devotee of God.

True devotion is self-surrender. Devotion does not consist so much in prayer, ecstatic chanting, or elaborate ritual worship, as it does in surrendering oneself to the Divine Will and doing one's allotted work calmly, in a spirit of divine worship, without complaining of anything, and accepting everything as sent by God for one's own quick evolution. The moment one adopts this attitude, then every difficulty, every obstacle, becomes a help to march ahead on the path of evolution. To a true devotee who has surrendered himself to the Lord, no task is difficult, no task is menial, no work is an obstacle on the path of his spiritual progress, for he does everything, knowing it to be the worship of God and fulfillment of the Divine Will. He thus maintains God-consciousness at all times.

Yoga is essentially the maintenance of an unbroken state of God-consciousness. True inner peace is not obtained by running away to the Himalayas. It is attained by having the correct understanding that every created thing is God, and that all work is divine worship.

VIII

Developing Moral Courage

by Meher Baba

If the inner life of an aspirant is to be harmonious and enlightened, he has to develop and express many divine qualities while engaged in his daily duties. Each quality by itself may not seem to be extremely important, but to consider it apart from its necessary relationship with other important qualities is not correct. In spiritual life all these qualities implement and support each other, and their interconnection is so vital that not one of them can be completely ignored without detriment to many other essential qualities. So, considered in its true function, each of these divine qualities turns out to be absolutely indispensable for a complete life.

Patience and Persistence

Every person is a rightful heir to the Truth. But he who would inherit it must be spiritually prepared, and this spiritual preparation sometimes takes several lives of patient and persistent effort. Therefore, one of the first requirements of an aspirant is to combine unfailing enthusiasm with unyielding patience. Once an individual is determined to realize the Truth, he finds that his path is beset with many difficulties, and there are very few who persist with steady courage till the very end. It is easy to give up the effort when one is confronted with obstacles. . . .

Spiritual effort demands not only physical endurance and courage but also unshrinking forbearance and unassailable moral courage.

Forbearance

The world is caught up in *māyā* and is addicted to false values. Therefore the ways of the world run counter to the standards the aspirant has set for himself. If he runs away from the world, that does not help him. He will again have to come back to the world to develop that quality which would enable him to face and accept the world as it is. Very often his path lies through the world that he has to serve in spite of not liking its ways. If the aspirant is to love and serve the world that does not understand him or is even intolerant toward him, he must develop infinite forbearance.

As the aspirant advances on the spiritual path, he acquires, through his contact with a Perfect Master, an increasingly deeper understanding of true love. This makes him painfully sensitive to the impact from outside actions that not only do not taste of love but actually bring him into contact with cold contempt, cynical callousness, agonizing antipathy, and unabating hatred. All these encounters try his forbearance to the utmost. Even the worldly person suffers in a world he occasionally finds indifferent or hostile, but he is more thick-skinned and his suffering is less acute. He does not expect anything much better from human nature and thinks that these things are inevitable and incurable. The aspirant, who has tasted a deeper love, knows the hidden possibilities in every soul. Thus his suffering is more acute because he feels the gulf between that which is and that which might have been, if only the world had even faintly appreciated the love he has begun to understand and cherish.

Self-Confidence

The task of forbearance would be easy if the aspirant could become reconciled to the ways of the world and accept them without challenge. Having seen the higher truths, however, it becomes his imperative duty to stand by them, even if the whole world opposes him. Loyalty to the higher truths of his own perception demands unshakable moral courage and readiness to face the criticism, the scorn, and even the hatred of those who have not yet begun to open up to these truths. Although in this uneven struggle he does get unfailing help from the Master and other aspirants, he has to develop the capacity to fight for these truths single-handedly, without relying upon external help all the time. This supreme moral courage can only come with supreme confidence in oneself and the Master. To love the world and serve it in the ways of the Masters is no game for the weak and fainthearted.

Freedom from Worry

Moral courage and self-confidence should be accompanied by freedom from worry. There are very few things in the mind that eat up as much energy as worry. It is one of the most difficult things not to worry about anything. Worry is experienced when things go wrong, and in relation to past happenings it is idle merely to wish that they might have been otherwise. The frozen past is what it is, and no amount of worrying is going to make it other than what it has been. Nonetheless, the limited ego-mind identifies itself with its past, gets entangled with it, and keeps alive the pangs of frustrated desires. Thus worry continues to grow into the mental life of a person until the ego-mind is burdened by the past.

Worry is also experienced in relation to the future, when this future is expected to be disagreeable in some way. In this case worry seeks to justify itself as a necessary part of the attempt to prepare for coping with the anticipated situations. But things can never be helped merely by worrying. Besides, many of the things that are anticipated never happen; or if they do occur, they turn out to be much more acceptable than they were expected to be. Worry is the product of feverish imagination working under the stimulus of desires. It is the living through of sufferings that are mostly of one's own creation. Worry has never done anyone any good; and it is very much worse than mere dissipation of energy, for it substantially curtails the joy and fullness of life.

Cheerfulness, Enthusiasm, and Equipoise

Among the many things the aspirant needs to cultivate, there are few that are as important as cheerfulness, enthusiasm, and equipoise. When the mind is gloomy, depressed, or disturbed, its actions are chaotic and binding. Hence arises the supreme need to maintain cheerfulness, enthusiasm, and equipoise under all circumstances. All these are rendered impossible unless the aspirant succeeds in eliminating worry from his life. Worry is a result of attachment to the past or to the anticipated future, and it always persists in some form or other until the mind is completely detached from everything.

One-Pointedness

Difficulties on the spiritual path can be overcome only if the aspirant has one-pointedness. If his energies are dissipated in worldly pursuits, the progress he makes is very slow. One-pointedness implies dispassion concerning all the allurements of the phenomenal world. The mind must turn away from all temptations, and complete control must be established over the senses. Thus control and dispassion are both necessary to attain one-pointedness in the search for true understanding.

The supreme condition for sure and steady progress on the path is the benefit of guidance from a Perfect Master. The Master gives just that guidance and help which is necessary according to the immediate needs of the aspirant. All the Master expects is that the aspirant will try his best for spiritual advancement. He does not expect immediate transformation of consciousness except where the ground has been previously made ready. Time is an important factor in spiritual advancement, as it is in all material endeavors. When the Master has given a spiritual push to the aspirant, he waits till the help thus given is completely assimilated by him. An overdose of spirituality always has an unhealthy reaction, particularly when it is inopportune. The Master therefore carefully selects the moment when his intervention is assured of maximum results; and having intervened, he waits with infinite patience till the aspirant really needs further help.

PART THREE

Reflections on Values

*Wisdom is knowing
what one ought to do next;
virtue is doing it.
Wisdom without virtue
is a weariness of the flesh.
Where thought does not go over into action,
there results spiritual constipation.*

Swami Ram Tirtha

We pray to God, we take His name, we meditate upon Him, but if we do not, at the same time, practice forgiveness, kindness, and compassion toward our fellow human beings, we shall not be able to approach God, we shall never be fit to receive His grace. The best way to make our actions acceptable to God is by making them self-less. We must do actions in a spirit of complete surrender to the Divine Will, feeling that it is by His prompting and by His inspiration that we are acting. In such actions themselves we must find joy and peace, without caring for the fruits.

We must be strictly moral in all that we do, be truthful and straightforward. As we practice such disciplines, our minds become purified and our prayers fruitful. It is then that our vision is widened, and in meditation our heart is opened to God who is the all-pervading Spirit. We then begin to feel the presence of God within us and we merge ourselves in Him, as the inner Truth and also as the outer life or expression of His universal existence. By living in accordance with this ideal, the purpose of our birth as human beings is fulfilled.

Swami Ramdas
Ramdas Speaks

IX

Revolution In Therapy

by Lewis M. Andrews

Modern psychology is on the verge of a transformation which may prove as important a turning point in the history of psychotherapy as relativity was to physics or DNA to biology. After nearly a century of doggedly refusing to acknowledge any possible connection between effective therapy and traditional ethical values, increasing numbers of practicing psychiatrists are choosing to describe their own patients' emotional problems in ethical, moral, and even spiritual terms.

And like those revolutions in physics and biology, the implications of this new "ethical" approach for the quality of everyday living extend well beyond the boundaries of professional theorizing. In the chapters to come [the author's book, *To Thine Own Self Be True*] we will see how ethical therapy is leading to dramatic advances in the treatment not only of major emotional problems such as depression, guilt, and fear, but of many related physical complaints as well.

As to my own interest in the therapeutic importance of values, I suppose I have never been quite comfortable with the tendency of modern academic psychologists to equate the purity of their science with the complete rejection of ethical tradition. One of my most vivid memories from my undergraduate years at Princeton was listening to a professor argue that a "good" psychologist had to be absolutely "value-free" in his approach, for any discussion of ethical discipline or moral responsibility would be admitting a degree of freedom which negated any hope of scientifically predicting human behavior. There was also the thinly veiled warning that legitimizing a subject so often associated with traditional religion would make psychology vulnerable to subversion by the worst kind of theological dogma and superstition.

Even then it seemed to me that my professor's fears were a bit exaggerated. Although treating patients as people capable of making independent ethical choices might conflict with some psychologists' dream of reducing man to a completely predictable biochemical machine, there was still plenty of room for valuable scientific research. One could measure, for example, whether habitually honest people are happier or more successful than their dishonest counterparts. Or how different ethical values are related to the incidence of various emotional disorders.

Of course, if there had been any hard evidence to support a "value-free" approach to psychotherapy, I probably would have given my professor's prescription more serious consideration. In point of fact, though, neither psychoanalysis nor behavior modification—the two most prominent psychiatric schools of that time—had ever really proven themselves very effective in alleviating patients' emotional problems. Indeed, what research had been done up until that point suggested that the long-term effect of conventional psychotherapies could just as easily be negative as positive,[1] even on patients who themselves were therapists.[2] (Today, psychoanalysis and behavior modification are still the leading schools of therapeutic thought, but the inability of either to distinguish itself in a meaningful way[3] is a problem that continues to haunt the profession.[4] As recently as January of 1985, Dr. Saul Levine, a Professor of Psychiatry at the University of Toronto, had to admit that "in spite of years of accumulated knowledge, well-controlled, reliable and valid studies of psychiatric success are still hard to come by."[5])

The threat of incorporating ethical choice into psychiatric treatment, I began to sense, was not that it would interfere with the possibility for useful scientific research, but that the human dignity and mystery implied by this approach would prevent the professional psychologist from feeling as superior as he might like to his patients, and to the "less sophisticated" layman in general. I also began to wonder if psychology's persistent allergy to any subject even faintly connected to traditional religion or philosophy might not be exactly the kind of dogmatic and negative thinking a "good" psychiatrist ought to be trying to cure.

Internal Transformation

How exactly I made the journey from this vague undergraduate dissatisfaction with the "value-free" bias of academic psychotherapy to finally embracing the traditional values of *honesty*, *tolerance*, and *intuitive self-reliance* as a primary form of treatment is a long story, combining more personal and professional experience than could easily be condensed. Yet, to the extent such evolutions can really be summarized, two incidents have always seemed particularly important.

The first happened over fifteen years ago while I was still in graduate school at Stanford. Through a series of circumstances I had gone into therapy with an unusually talented and iconoclastic Palo Alto psychologist named Jon Davidson. I don't remember what problem I had presented on this particular day, only that I was trying to make a case for telling some kind of white lie.

"Do you really want to do this to yourself?" Jon interrupted provocatively.

"Do what?" I replied blankly.

"Lie," he answered. "Don't you realize that by trying to manipulate somebody else you're only going to hurt yourself."

"Oh well . . . maybe if you believe in some kind of afterlife justice. . . ."

"No, no!," Jon continued in his animated way. "I'm talking about right *now*, what you're going to feel *today*!"

After some further discussion, I finally realized what Jon was getting at. Lying, if I took the trouble to be aware of it, was really a terrible psychological state. My vision dimmed, my pulse quickened anxiously, and there was a noticeable loss of contact with the outside world, all this in addition to any long-term effects of such stress.

Indeed, the more I experimented with disciplining my deceitful impulses in the days and months that followed—forsaking the temptation to manipulate other people's feelings and stating my real intentions without the usual rationalizations—the more confident and peaceful I began to feel. The improvement in my social life was particularly noticeable. After months of living a rather lonely and isolated campus life, I suddenly found myself with a new girlfriend and full weekend schedules of skiing and tennis.

The second pivotal incident in the development of my thought occurred roughly ten years ago while I was driving back to California from a trip East. It lasted no longer than a second, though it can fairly be said that the emotional turmoil leading up to it, including guilt over a girlfriend's recent abortion and the mishandling of some writing projects, had gone on for some time.

The time was about an hour after dark when I noticed what seemed to be a flash in an otherwise clear sky. At first I thought I had seen lightning, but quickly realized that the flash was an incredible internal transformation. Suddenly, after years of doubting and uncertainty, I had accepted the existence of an inner self—a *soul* if I dared use that most unpsychiatric of words—whose knowledge and wisdom extended well beyond my biological conception of brain power.

I already knew that reports of such inner realizations were quite common in people rebounding from emotional stress—Gallup polls suggest that as many as 70 percent of all Americans can expect a similar experience at least once during their lives.[6] But I was quite unprepared for the lasting authority of the event or for the unavoidable intellectual implication that many of the intuitions I had so often dismissed as irrelevant fantasies or wishful thinking—my hunches, instincts, and "gut" feelings— might actually represent a higher form of wisdom.

Spontaneous Intuition

The more I dared to test this proposition, however, the more truth there seemed to be to it. Following an intuitive impulse to organize some seemingly trivial part of my life, for example, or to investigate some oddly intriguing subject I'd happened to hear about, would prove just days or weeks later to have an unexpected utility. I would also find, when hiring someone for a job, that the briefest personal impression was a far better predictor of his or her performance than any recommendation or resume. Even the impulse to call a distant relative or contact an old friend I hadn't seen in years would turn out to demonstrate exceptionally good timing.

Indeed, my experience with trusting my intuition was so successful that I found myself in a strange quandary. In the months and years following my discussions with Jon Davidson, I had become convinced that certain ethical restraints, particularly honesty and the willingness to curb judgmental tendencies, were absolutely essential to personal happiness; yet now it was becoming clear that being more spontaneous also had something to do with it. How could somebody believe in both discipline and spontaneous intuition at the same time?

Fortunately, it soon became apparent that these seemingly opposite approaches to life were quite compatible, and indeed, had the surprising effect of reinforcing each other. This is to say that the more I learned to trust my intuitive wisdom, the less I felt I had to judge and manipulate other people. Similarly, it was my willingness to be more open and tolerant with others that seemed to strengthen and clarify my intuitive perceptions. The juxtaposition of ethical discipline and intuitive self-reliance proved not to be a psychological paradox after all, but two aspects of the same therapeutic process.

Reexamining Conventional Psychology

In the decade since that remarkable drive back to California, I have had many opportunities to share these conclusions with scores of professional friends and colleagues, and each year the response becomes so increasingly sympathetic that what at first seemed like a solitary undergraduate's futile rebellion against a "value-free" psychiatric establishment now appears as but one expression of a much broader movement. The continued inability of conventional therapies to produce anything approximating a cure, coupled with a broader cultural interest in traditional values, has created a situation where even the most stubbornly avowed psychoanalyst or behavior modifier will admit, in the relaxed atmosphere of late night conversation, that no patient has ever really been healed who has not adopted a more spiritual point of view.

Indeed, I don't think it is a coincidence that as of this writing the board of directors of the American Psychiatric Association is facing widespread resistance from its own rank-and-file members to its attempt to publish an official manual of recommended treatments for emotional disorders. It is one thing to require would-be psychiatrists to study "value-free" theories in order to get a license to practice, quite another to force them to continue using these theories on innocent patients with real problems.

Of course, the most important question of all is not how I personally stumbled upon the therapeutic wisdom of traditional values, or why I believe so many working professionals will be openly supportive of the ethical techniques described in this book, but how someone currently suffering the throes of depression, guilt, or some other emotional problem can begin to apply this emerging therapy to his or her particular situation. Conventional psychology's long neglect of this topic has so debased our everyday language that even the person who senses the need to be more honest, tolerant, or intuitive can easily get lost in semantic confusion over the meaning of such words. The seemingly paradoxical nature of traditional values—the simultaneous belief in ethical discipline coupled with a faith in the wisdom of spontaneous expression—only appears to compound the problem.

Fortunately, the therapeutic use of traditional values proves surprisingly straightforward once we understand a few basic concepts. In this respect, the motivated layman, whose only concern is his own happiness and the well-being of loved ones, has a distinct advantage over many academic psychologists who have made a career out of defending psychoanalysis, behavior modification, or some other "value-free" point of view.

Approached with an open mind and a bit of courage, ethical therapy can provide lasting relief from a wide variety of emotional problems. The only prerequisite is some historical sense of how ethical therapy, whose effectiveness has been obvious for the better part of the last two thousand years, could have become so thoroughly obscured to modern eyes—and a willingness to question the sorry assumptions that still cloud conventional psychiatric wisdom.

FOOTNOTES:

[1] H. Stupp, et al., *Psychotherapy for Better or Worse: the Problem of Negative Effects.*
[2] P. Buckley, et al., *Psychotherapists View Their Personal Therapy.*
[3] M. Parloff, *Can Psychotherapy Research Guide the Policy Maker?*
[4] M. Goldfried, *Toward the Delineation of Therapeutic Change Principles.*
[5] S. Levine, *Who Should Do Psychotherapy?* p. 61.
[6] *Religion in America*: 1982, p.7.

X

Values in the Family

Aasha Reddy

It had been a long and hot day at the office for Arvind. Everything appeared to be going wrong since he started work in the morning. He had an argument with a colleague on trivials, he could not locate some important files in time and, moreover, he had developed a headache. He was longing for the day to be over, because at the end of it was something he could look forward to with pleasure—his home, sweet home.

School was something Divya always enjoyed going to, but today was an exception. She was pulled up by her teacher for something she had not done, her best friend simply ignored her, and she was feeling miserable. Finally, it was the last bell, and with a sense of relief Divya packed up her bag. There was something she could look forward to with pleasure—her home, sweet home.

What is it that makes a home a *sweet* home? Is it the beautiful exterior, the garden, the nice furniture, kitchen gadgets? No, it is people—the parents, the elders, the children and the pets—who make a home sweet. It is the warmth, intimacy, and laughter they share that brings joy and happiness into a home. But this kind of harmony does not come about automatically. It needs effort, mutual respect, and a willingness to share common interests, sympathies, and pleasures. In other words, it needs the observance of a value system. According to A. J. Cronin, the famous British author, "Through the centuries the family has taken foremost place, not only in the safeguarding of morality, but in the evolution of human culture. Wherever the family flourishes in a state of vigor and unity, there will be found a strong and sound society. In an era of fear and restlessness, when people ringed by hostile forces feel isolated in a dark loneliness, the family is their main hope for self-preservation, for maintaining human dignity and the decencies of life."

Integrity

Perhaps the most important value a family has to cherish is integrity. It is impossible to imagine any livable society, let alone a family, without it. Put simply, integrity demands that we always mean what we say and say what we mean, and that we do not cheat or lie to one another. It implies that the affection we profess for anything is genuine and the praise we give is honest. It is a quality which has to be inculcated in children while they are still small. This is something that cannot be taught, but has to be shown. We teach integrity by the way we live ourselves. A small boy was wrongly accused by his teacher of telling a lie. The boy retorted proudly, "Our family doesn't lie." Integrity gives one the strength to walk through life with one's head held high.

Children are great imitators and have a natural tendency to do as their parents do. This places a heavy responsibility on parents to lead their lives in such a way that they are walking, talking examples of a set of values which they wish to impart to their children. Many are the times when children are told not to tell lies, but the very next moment they are confused to find their parents asking them to tell a caller that they are not at home. Isn't it a common experience to hear a child say, "My father told me to tell you that he is not at home?"

There is only one real magic in this life that can move mountains and turn dreams into reality. That magic is "Believing in yourself." Only those who believe in themselves and their capacity to meet challenges are able to face life with courage. Almost anyone can achieve anything if only he believes in himself.

Austrian tennis player Thomas Muster won the French Open title a few months back. He has also been acknowledged as the best clay-court player of the year. A few years ago, he was involved in a serious accident and medical opinion was that he might not be able to walk, let alone play tennis. But through sheer grit, determination, and self-effort, he has bounced back to the top of his profession. In the words of Swami Vivekananda, "The old religions said that he was an atheist who did not believe in God. The new religion says that he is an atheist who does not believe in himself."

Self-Reliance

Can parents really do anything to encourage self-reliance in a child? Yes, the secret lies in watching to see where a child's innate skills or talents lie and gently nurturing them. We should listen lovingly and respectfully to a child's plans and hopes, however naive they may seem and, wherever possible, help to make them come true.

Kahlil Gibran, the well-known Lebanese mystic, has expressed this so beautifully in his masterpiece, *The Prophet*.

> You may give them [your children] your love
> but not your thoughts.
> You may house their bodies but not their souls.
> For their souls dwell in the house of tomorrow, which you
> cannot visit, not even in your dreams.
> You may strive to be like them, but seek not to make them like
> you. For life goes not backward nor tarries with yesterday.
> You are the bows from which your children as living arrows
> are sent forth.

Today's children are exposed to many anxiety-causing experiences and caught amidst too many choices. When your daughter comes to you with her fears, listen to her and assure her that it is all right to be scared and that she is not alone in feeling this way. Then help her constructively to overcome them. Making fun of her in such situations can cause irreparable harm. Childhood fears are a part of growing up.

Pessimism, fear, and gloom are highly contagious. In a home filled with these, a child's self-confidence can hardly grow or even survive. If, however, the atmosphere at home is one of love, contentment, and laughter, the child develops the ability to look past dark times to brighter ones, to believe that questions do have answers, that challenges can be met, and that problems can be solved. This builds character and endurance, and so the uncertainties of life appear less frightening.

A bit of humor is almost indispensable and helps bring family and friends closer. Humor can help relieve tension and give a new perspective to an otherwise grim and hopeless situation. It enables us, even in trying times, to smile and wink at life.

Open your child's life to the world of books. Read to him at least for a few minutes every day. Is it hard, in a day packed with twenty-four hours, to spend at least fifteen or twenty minutes to read to your child? Get your child hooked on to reading and he or she will never be alone again.

Compassion and Concern

Children are naturally sensitive to pain and suffering in others. If the climate in the home is one of compassion and concern for others, this sensitivity gets strengthened. We celebrate the birthdays of our children with great enthusiasm and expense. How wonderful it would be if on the same day some money is also spent on fulfilling the needs of the less fortunate!

We spend so much of our time having "a good time" that we become insensitive to the needs of others. Taking your little son on a monthly visit to an orphanage, any home for the less privileged, or animal shelters will expose him to the values of com passion, love, and sharing. Such experiences have the most subtle, profound, and enduring influence upon the physical, moral, and emotional health of the child. He will experience the joy of giving and sharing and will develop the capacity to love and to feel.

There is a tendency among some women today to downplay the role of a traditional mother in favor of a career. We should be aware, however, that there are many women who enjoy being a wife and mother, not because they are incompetent to pursue a career, but because they derive greater satisfaction from these. According to C. E. Barker, an analytical psychotherapist, "One of the tragedies of this modern science-soaked society with its obsession for technology, is that mothers now tend to think their contribution to the world is of little account. . . . It assumes that motherhood is a temporary affliction imposed on women which severely interferes with their fight to show themselves as good as men. . . . Alas, such women have no idea that the job of being a mother and offering a tiny human being her identity, warmth, protective love, and tenderness determines the health, well-being, security, stability, and sanity of the coming generation."

Barker continues, "A generation of good 'mothering' would make an unbelievable contribution toward producing a civilization that would work for stability and peace."

Swami Vivekananda sums up the greatness of motherhood in simple words: "The position of the mother is the highest in the world, for it is the one place in which to learn and exercise the greatest unselfishness."

One of the most reassuring and stabilizing experiences in a child's life is the deep love and friendship between the parents. The best way for a father to convey his affection to his children is through the love and understanding he gives to their mother and vice versa. A child's expectations from a father are simple— love and time. What children most remember about their father is his simple presence.

The greatest gift that parents can give to a child is a sense of discipline. Children will benefit by discipline only when it is exacted fairly and firmly and against a background of love. Studies have shown that adults who had been punished in childhood look back in anger, whereas those who had been disciplined look back with gratitude.

Appreciation for Life

A respect for life, for time—ours and that of others—a respect for law, traffic rules, public property, an awareness of the importance of a clean, green, and healthy environment are essential values which need to be implanted in the minds of children, with parents as prime examples. For instance, it is a common sight in Germany to see this signboard at pedestrian crossings: "Cross only by green light; set an example to your children."

In our daily lives, routine as they may seem, we are very often touched by rare and charming things. The sweetness lies in being able to recognize and appreciate them. We should be able to appreciate little gestures of kindness and the simple beauty of things around us. And above all, the world is about people and the only way we can mean anything to another human being is to share our feelings, and show them that we care. All our feelings, appreciation, and good intentions don't mean a thing unless we express them.

Our lives will be so much richer and fuller if we remain young, in the sense that the child within us is never lost. We should grow in all the traits of a child—questioning, curiosity, appreciation, laughter, open-mindedness. It is not the years but attitudes that make a person seem young or old.

The most precious legacy that we can pass on to our children is a strong religious faith, a belief that there exists a loving God, who cares for us and is ever available to support and help us in times of need. It is the trust that God never abandons us and even in the darkest hour His light still shines to lead us on. This inner conviction will give our children great strength and keep them going in moments of crises.

It is not human society alone which has a value system. There is a particular kind of rodent in Scandinavia called the Lemming. Lemmings live on top of mountains. Whenever there is an abnormal increase in their population leading to a shortage of food, a certain number of them run down the mountains and drown themselves in the sea. This is witnessed by a large number of people year after year. Scientists are baffled at this remarkable phenomenon. It can be explained only by assuming that the Lemmings respect the value of self-sacrifice and concern for fellow creatures. We are equally amazed at the socio-structure and order exhibited by the ants and the bees, which would not be possible without a value system of their own. We humans should be humble enough to recognize this fact and try to emulate them for a harmonious living.

XI

Values of a Sadhu

by Swami Vidyatmananda

The American writer Edith Wharton is reported to have said, "I don't believe in God, but I do believe in His saints."

At first glance, an apparently flippant statement but understandable upon mature reflection. You have only to think about it to see that Edith Wharton's is a sentiment with which many would agree. The concept of God is remote—available mainly through scriptural reports and the claims of theology. But the concrete evidence of living, functioning saintliness—which we can see in an occasional advanced human being—is immediately believable and powerfully convincing. Such human saintliness may be the best and only Godliness that some of us are capable of perceiving—the Ultimate Being more available through his saintly particularities than through Itself! Godly qualities manifested in a human being offer the best demonstration of the God that we cannot otherwise see. For most of us, a living, functioning saint is more precious than a divine concept sought mainly through an effort of imagination.

Thus the enormous value of His saints, of which a primary example is what we call a *sadhu*—a holy man (or woman) whom we are occasionally fortunate to find in our midst. In Vedanta the word *sadhu* is a general term meaning spiritual person. The word comes from the Sanskrit *sadh,* a verb meaning "to lead to fulfillment." He (or she) is very holy and at the same time reassuringly human.

I have known and worked with a real *sadhu*. And for this experience I shall be grateful forever. I don't say that I don't believe in God, as Edith Wharton says she does not, but like her I find the Divine more easily accessible in His saints. My conception of *sadhu* values comes from this experience—what qualities I saw manifested in my *sadhu*. I shall try to give a description in such a way as to reveal what these values are, expressed in him.

Availability

The primary quality I would cite is *availability*. My *sadhu* was open to everybody whether they were easy and attractive or not. He once told me that he had at a certain moment decided to make as many friends during his lifetime as possible, and he made good his intention. My *sadhu* had developed a sunny, permissive personality, one sensed that one could unguardedly tell him anything and that he would be interested. Moreover he would not judge or condemn, and he would keep one's confidences. Although being essentially of a shy disposition and unassertive in most fields of activity, my *sadhu* was uncharacteristically aggressive in attracting and cultivating new contacts. He was especially interested in those individuals having adjustment difficulties—the misfits, the friendless, the inept. And how they did respond to his advances! I teased him by labeling him an obsessive collector of wounded birds.

Besides having to conduct continual personal interviews, my *sadhu*'s availability resulted in an enormous correspondence—long and complicated recitations of personal problems expressed in difficult handwritings and several languages. Once when my *sadhu* confessed that he was overwhelmed by the flow of letters I reminded him that his ambition had been to acquire as many friends as possible. "Here is your result!" I asked him what it was that all those people wrote about. His answer was: "It's very simple. They want to tell somebody something that is interesting to them, and they assume that that something is interesting to the person to whom they are writing. So I try to reply, even a few lines. Generally not giving advice, but just being friendly and encouraging. It gives them comfort."

I had thus a daily demonstration of something my own guru tried to inculcate in me and which I was so slow to learn: "Feel for others, my child," he often entreated. "You must learn to feel for others."

Positiveness

The second *sadhu* value my *sadhu* adhered to was *positiveness*. He genuinely believed in the potential perfectibility of everyone. The quality of not criticizing was firmly established as a part of his personality. When someone did something clearly unwise or obviously wrong, his usual observation was: "But he's like that, that's his nature. What can he do?" And then he would probably add, "But he will surely change." That's the final line of the few negative assessments of people I ever heard my *sadhu* utter: "He will suffer from the course he is taking, and suffering will force him to change." How many times I heard these words from him! "He (or she) will surely change." He never looked at people according to the weaknesses which they manifested at a given time. Rather, he considered them as, certainly not bad, but merely immature. He believed in the future spiritual success of everybody he came in contact with, and it was this belief in them that attracted so many people to him.

Try as I did, I could never manage to involve my *sadhu* in the behavioral shortcomings of others in the community. Any complaint was turned aside blandly. "Moods change." His policy when he was himself scolded or complained against was to remain silent. Just to sit silently until the other had run out of words. So no self-defense, just silence. This response had the effect of disarming the assailant and finally forcing him to desist, defeated. My *sadhu* was impossible to quarrel with. Once, however, when I was really irritated about something he had done I made up my mind to have things out with him. He listened in silence to my angry words and then answered calmly: "You know you are angry. So your reason is disturbed. We'll wait a little while for the emotion to go and then we'll discuss the matter like the good friends we are."

I see now that only a saintly man—a *sadhu*—could act in the ways I have described. The early uncertainty I felt in dealing with a man so different from anyone I had ever met before turned into admiration—even emulation. I tried to learn to follow the same modes of behavior myself. "Be patient, be positive, and let things work out. Who can tell what is good, what is ultimately bad, what is progress, what is success? It all depends. Progress is so individual. Don't come to conclusions. There are so many criteria, spiritual unfoldment is too subtle to analyze. Who knows how God works? Who knows what God wants?"

For my *sadhu* the purpose of religion was to produce a change in the individual who practiced it—a change of character, a change in his habitual reactions, a fundamental change in that person's very thought-patterns. A genuinely spiritual person is one who has learned to live at peace with oneself, who lives in peace with others, and who copes competently with the vagaries of the everyday world in which human beings are forced to live. My *sadhu* was not impressed by claims concerning mystical experiences or celestial emotions when not accompanied by a corresponding amelioration in the individual's lifestyle. "Have you become a mature person?" would have been his question. Spiritual practice, properly done, should transform an individual into something of a sage, as it had transformed him.

I have said that the *sadhu* value which I beheld in my *sadhu* were *availability* and *positiveness*. He practiced them conscientiously, and his effect on those fortunate to know him was generative. For many individuals my *sadhu* was the only God they cared to know, the grace he transmitted was sufficient for them. Whether or not they would be able ultimately to believe in God as God, in any case they had His Saint as pre-instructor. We may suppose that these *sadhu* values were God's means of bringing those lovers of my *sadhu* eventually to Himself.

XII

My Steps Toward
Inner Peace

by Peace Pilgrim

As I looked about the world, so much of it impoverished, I became increasingly uncomfortable about having so much while my brothers and sisters were starving. Finally I had to find another way. The turning point came when, in desperation and out of a very deep seeking for a meaningful way of life, I walked all alone one night through the woods. I came to a moonlit glade and prayed.

I felt a complete willingness, without any reservations, to give my life—to dedicate my life—to service. "Please use me!" I prayed to God. And a great peace came over me.

I tell you it's a point of no return. After that, you can never go back to completely self-centered living.

And so I went into the second phase of my life. I began to live to *give* what I could, instead of to *get* what I could, and I entered a new and wonderful world. My life began to be meaningful. I attained the great blessing of good health; I haven't had an ache or pain, a cold or headache since. (Most illness, you know, is psychologically induced.) From that time on, I have known that my life work would be for peace—that it would cover the *whole peace picture*: peace among nations, peace among groups, peace among individuals, and the very, very important inner peace. However, there's a great deal of difference between being *willing* to give your life and actually *giving* your life, and for me fifteen years of preparation and inner seeking lay between.

Lower and Higher Self

I was not far down the spiritual road when I became acquainted with what the psychologists refer to as ego and conscience, which I call the lower self and the higher self, or the self-centered nature and the God-centered nature. It's as though we have two selves or natures or two wills with two contrary viewpoints.

Your lower self sees things from the viewpoint of your physical well-being only—your higher self considers your psychological or spiritual well-being. Your lower self sees you as the center of the universe—your higher self sees you as a cell in the body of humanity. When you are governed by your lower self you are selfish and materialistic, but insofar as you follow the promptings of your higher self you will see things realistically and find harmony within yourself and others.

The body, mind, and emotions are instruments which can be used by either the self-centered nature or the God-centered nature. The self-centered nature uses these instruments, yet it is never fully able to control them, so there is a constant struggle. They can only be fully controlled by the God-centered nature.

When the God-centered nature takes over, you have found inner peace. Until that time comes, a partial control can be gained through discipline. It can be discipline imposed from without through early training which has become a part of the subconscious side of the self-centered nature. It can be discipline undertaken voluntarily: self-discipline. Now, if you are doing things you know you shouldn't do and don't really want to do, you certainly lack discipline. I recommend spiritual growing—and in the meantime self-discipline.

During the spiritual growing up period the inner conflict can be more or less stormy. Mine was about average. The self-centered nature is a very formidable enemy and it struggles fiercely to retain its identity. It defends itself in a cunning manner and should not be regarded lightly. It knows the weakest spots of your armor and attempts a confrontation when one is least aware. During these periods of attack, maintain a humble stature and be intimate with none but the guiding whisper of your higher self.

The higher self has been given many wonderful names by religious leaders, some calling the higher governing power the *inner light*, or the *indwelling Christ*. When Jesus said, "The Kingdom of God is within you," he was obviously referring to the higher self. In another place it says, "Christ in you, your hope of glory, the indwelling Christ." Jesus was called the Christ because his life was governed by this higher governing power.

When I talk about my steps toward inner peace, I talk about them in a framework, but there's nothing arbitrary about the number of steps. They can be expanded; they can be contracted. This is just a way of talking about the subject, but this is important: the steps toward inner peace are not taken in any certain order. The first step for one may be the last step for another. So just take whatever steps seem easiest for you, and as you take a few steps, it will become easier for you to take a few more. In this area we can really share. None of you may feel guided to walk a pilgrimage, and I'm not trying to inspire you to do so. But in the field of finding harmony in our own lives, we can share. And I suspect that when you hear me give some of the steps toward inner peace, you will recognize them as steps that you also have taken.

Right Attitude

I would like to mention some preparations that were required of me. The first preparation is to take *a right attitude toward life*. This means, stop being an escapist! Stop being a surface liver who stays right in the froth of the surface. There are millions of these people, and they never find anything really worthwhile. Be willing to face life squarely and get down beneath the surface of life where the verities and realities are to be found. That's what we are doing here now.

There is the whole matter of having a meaningful attitude toward the problems that life may set before you. If only you could see the whole picture, if you knew the whole story, you would realize that no problem ever comes to you that does not have a purpose in your life, that cannot contribute to your inner growth. When you perceive this, you will recognize that problems are opportunities in disguise. If you did not face problems, you would just drift through life. It is through solving problems in accordance with the highest light we have that inner growth is attained. Now, collective problems must be solved by us collectively, and no one finds inner peace who avoids doing his or her share in the solving of collective problems, like world disarmament and world peace. So let us always think about these problems together and talk about them together, and collectively work toward their solutions.

In Harmony with Divine Laws

The second preparation has to do with *bringing our lives into harmony with the laws that govern this universe.* Created are not only the worlds and the beings, but also the laws that govern them. Applying both in the physical realm and in the psychological realm, these laws govern human conduct. Insofar as we are able to understand and bring our lives into harmony with these laws, our lives will be in harmony. Insofar as we disobey these laws, we create difficulties for ourselves by our disobedience. We are our own worst enemies. If we are out of harmony through ignorance, we suffer somewhat; but if we know better and are still out of harmony, then we suffer a great deal. Suffering pushes us toward obedience.

I recognized that there are some well-known, little understood, and seldom practiced laws that we must live by if we wish to find peace within or without. Included are the laws that evil can only be overcome by good; that only good means can attain a good end; that those who do unloving things hurt themselves spiritually.

These laws are the same for all human beings and must be obeyed before harmony can prevail.

So I got busy on a very interesting project. This was to live all the good things I believed in. I did not confuse myself by trying to take them all at once, but rather if I was doing something that I knew I shouldn't be doing I stopped doing it and I always made a quick relinquishment. That's the easy way. Tapering off is long and hard. And if I was not doing something that I knew I should be doing, I got busy on that. It took the living quite a while to catch up with the believing, but of course it can, and now if I believe something, I live it. Otherwise it would be perfectly meaningless. As I lived according to the *highest light* I had, I discovered that *other light* was given; that I opened myself to receiving more light as I lived the light I had.

Learning to Listen

There is a third preparation that has to do with something which is unique for every human life, because every one of us has *a special place in the Life Pattern*, and no two people have exactly the same part to play in God's plan. There is a guidance which comes from within to all who will listen. Through this guidance each one will feel drawn to some part in the scheme of things.

God's laws can be known from within, but they can also be learned from without, as they have been spoken of by all great religious teachers. God's *guidance* can only be known from within.

We must remain open to God's guidance. God never guides

us to break divine law, and if such a negative guidance comes to us we can be sure it is not from God. It is up to us to keep our lives steadfastly in harmony with divine law, which is the same for all of us. Only insofar as we remain in harmony with divine law do good things come to us.

' When you come into this world your jobs in the divine plan are there. They just need to be realized and lived. If you do not yet know where you fit, I suggest that you try seeking it in receptive silence. I used to walk amid the beauties of nature, just receptive and silent, and wonderful insights would come to me.

You begin to do your part in the Life Pattern by doing all of the good things you feel motivated toward, even though they are just little good things at first. You give these priority in your life over all the superficial things that customarily clutter human lives.

Every morning I thought of God and thought of things I might do that day to be of service to God's children. I looked at every situation I came into to see if there was anything I could do there to be of service. I did as many good things as I could each day, not forgetting the importance of a pleasant word and a cheery smile. I prayed about things that seemed too big for me to handle—and right prayer motivates to right action.

I was filled with a runaway enthusiasm to help others, and one could argue that when I solved so many problems for others I was depriving them of the spiritual growth problem-solving brings. I soon realized I had to leave some good works for others to do and be blessed by.

In the beginning I helped people in simple ways with errands, gardening projects, and by reading to them. I spent some time in the private homes of the elderly and the recuperating ill, assisting them to overcome their various ailments. I worked with troubled teenagers, the psychologically disturbed, and the physically and mentally handicapped. My motives were pure and much of my work did have a positive and good effect. I used what I call spiritual therapy: I found all the good things that those I worked with wanted to do, and I helped them to do those things. There were some who became too attached to me and I had to work on breaking the attachment.

My lack of expertise was more than offset by the love I extended to others. When love fills your life all limitations are gone. The medicine this sick world needs so badly is love.

I also did some volunteer work for the American Friends Service Committee, the Women's International League for Peace and Freedom, and the Fellowship of Reconciliation—over a period of at least ten years, off and on.

There are those who know and do not do. This is very sad. In this materialistic age we have such a false criterion by which to measure success. We measure it in terms of dollars, in terms of material things. But happiness and inner peace do not lie in that direction. If you *know* but do not *do*, you are a very unhappy person indeed.

Simplification of Life

There is a fourth preparation. It is *the simplification of life*, to bring inner and outer well-being, psychological and material well-being, into harmony in your life. This was made very easy for me. Just after I dedicated my life to service, I felt that I could no longer accept *more* than I need while others in the world have *less* than they need. This moved me to bring my life down to *need level*. I thought it would be difficult. I thought it would entail a great many hardships, but I was quite wrong. Instead of hardships, I found a wonderful sense of peace and joy, and a conviction that unnecessary possessions are only unnecessary burdens.

During this period I was able to meet my expenses on ten dollars a week, dividing my budget into two categories. I allocated $6.50 for food and incidentals and $3.50 for lodging.

Now I do not mean that needs are all the same. Your needs may be much greater than mine. For instance, if you have a family, you would need the stability of a family center for your children. But I do mean that anything beyond need—and need sometimes includes things beyond physical needs, too—anything beyond need tends to become burdensome. If you have it, you have to take care of it!

There is great freedom in simplicity of living, and after I began to feel this, I found harmony in my life between inner and outer well-being. There is a great deal to be said about such harmony, not only for an individual life but also for the life of a society. It's because as a world we have gotten ourselves so far out of harmony, so way off on the material side, that when we discover something like nuclear energy we are still capable of putting it into a bomb and using it to kill people! This is because our inner well-being lags so far behind our outer well-being. The valid research for the future is on the *inner* side, on the spiritual side, so that we will be able to bring these two into balance—and so that we will know how to use well the outer well-being we already have.

XIII

The Practice
of Virtues

by Benjamin Franklin

I wished to live without committing any fault at any time; I
would conquer all that either natural inclination, custom, or
company might lead me into. As I knew, or thought I knew, what
was right and wrong, I did not see why I might not do the one and
avoid the other. But I soon found I had undertaken a task of more
difficulty than I had imagined. While my attention was taken up
and care employed in guarding against one fault, I was often
surprised by another. Habit took the advantage of inattention.
Inclination was sometimes too strong for reason. I concluded at
length that the mere speculative conviction that it was our interest to be completely virtuous was not sufficient to prevent our
slipping, and that the contrary habits must be broken and good
ones acquired and established before we can have any depen-
dence on a steady, uniform rectitude of conduct. For this purpose I therefore contrived the following method.

In the various enumerations of the moral virtues I had met
with in my reading, I found the catalogue more or less numerous, as different writers included more or fewer ideas under the
same name. *Temperance*, for example, was by some confined
to eating and drinking, while by others it was extended to mean
the moderating of every other pleasure, appetite, inclination,
or passion, bodily or mental, even to our avarice and ambition.

I proposed to myself, for the sake of clearness, to use rather more names with fewer ideas annexed to each, than a few names with more ideas; and I included under thirteen names of virtues all that at the time occurred to me as necessary or desirable, and annexed to each a short precept which fully expressed the extent I gave to its meaning.

Thirteen Virtues

These names of virtues with their precepts were:

1. *Temperance*: Eat not to dullness. Drink not to elevation;

2. *Silence*: Speak not but what may benefit others or yourself. Avoid trifling conversation;

3. *Order*: Let all your things have their places. Let each part of your business have its time;

4. *Resolution*: Resolve to perform what you ought. Perform without fail what you resolve;

5. *Frugality*: Make no expense but to do good to others or yourself, that is, waste nothing;

6. *Industry*: Lose no time. Be always employed in something useful. Cut off all unnecessary actions;

7. *Sincerity*: Use no hurtful deceit. Think innocently and justly; and, if you speak, speak accordingly;

8. *Justice*: Wrong none by doing injuries or omitting the benefits that are your duty;

9. *Moderation*: Avoid extremes. Forbear resenting injuries so much as you think they deserve;

10. *Cleanliness*: Tolerate no uncleanness in body, clothes, or habitation;

11. *Tranquility*: Be not disturbed at trifles or at accidents common or unavoidable;

12. *Chastity*: Rarely use venery but for health or offspring, never to dullness, weakness, or the injury of your own or another's peace or reputation;

13. *Humility*: Imitate Jesus and Socrates;

My intention being to acquire the *habitude* of all these virtues, I judged it would be well not to distract my attention by attempting the whole at once, but to fix it on one of them at a time, and when I should be master of that, then to proceed to another, and so on, till I should have gone through the thirteen. And as the previous acquisition of some might facilitate the acquisition of certain others, I arranged them with that view as they stand above. *Temperance* first, as it tends to procure that coolness and clearness of head which is so necessary where constant vigilance was to be kept up, and guard maintained against the unremitting attraction of ancient habits, and the force of perpetual temptations. This being acquired and established, *Silence* would be more easy, and my desire being to gain knowledge at the same time that I improved in virtue, and considering that in conversation it was obtained rather by the use of the ear than of the tongue, and therefore wishing to break a habit I was getting into of prattling, punning, and joking, which only made me acceptable to trifling company, I gave *Silence* the second place. This and the next, *Order*, I expected would allow me more time for attending to my projects and my studies. *Resolution*, once become habitual, would keep me firm in my endeavors to obtain all the subsequent virtues; *Frugality* and *Industry*, freeing me from my remaining debt and, producing affluence and independence, would make the practice of *Sincerity* and *Justice* easier. Conceiving then that agreeable to the advice of Pythagoras in his Golden Verses, daily examination would be necessary, I contrived the following method for conducting that examination.

Practical Implementation

I made a little book in which I allotted a page for each of the virtues. I ruled each page with red ink so as to have seven columns, one for each day of the week, marking each column with a letter for the day. I crossed these columns with thirteen red lines, marking the beginning of each line with the first letter of one of the virtues, on which line, and in its proper column, I might mark, by a little black spot, every fault I found upon examination to have been committed respecting that virtue upon that day. I determined to give a week's strict attention to each of the virtues successively. Thus, in the first week, my great guard was to avoid even the least offense against *Temperance*, leaving the other virtues to their ordinary chance, only marking every evening the faults of the day. Thus, if in the first week I could keep my first line marked "T" clear of spots, I supposed the habit of that virtue so much strengthened and its opposite weakened that I might venture extending my attention to include the next, and for the following week keep both lines clear of spots. Proceeding thus to the last, I could go through a complete course in thirteen weeks, and four courses in a year. And like him who, having a garden to weed, does not attempt to eradicate all the bad herbs at once, which would exceed his reach and his strength, but works on one of the beds at a time, and having accomplished the first, proceeds to a second, so I should have (I hoped) the encouraging pleasure of seeing on my pages the progress I made in virtue, by clearing successively my lines of their spots, till in the end, by a number of courses, I should be happy in viewing a clean book after a thirteen weeks' daily examination.

My little book had for its motto these lines from Addison's Cato:

Here will I hold: if there is a power above us,
(And that there is, all Nature cries aloud
Thro' all her works) he must delight in virtue,
And that which he delights in must be happy.

Another from the proverbs of Solomon speaking of wisdom or virtue:

Length of days is in her right hand, and in her left hand riches and honors; her ways are ways of pleasantness, and all her paths are peace. (III:16,17)

And conceiving God to be the fountain of wisdom, I thought it right and necessary to solicit His assistance for obtaining it. To this end I formed the following little prayer, which was prefixed to my tables of examination for daily use.

> O Powerful Goodness, bountiful Father, merciful Guide! Increase in me that wisdom which discovers my truest interests. Strengthen my resolutions to perform what that wisdom dictates. Accept my kind offices to Thy other children, as the only return in my power for Thy continual favors to me.

I also sometimes used a little prayer which I took from Thompson's Poems:

> Father of light and life, thou Good supreme
> Oh, teach me what is good, teach me thy Self.
> Save me from folly, vanity and vice,
> From every low pursuit, and fill my soul
> With knowledge, conscious peace, and virtue pure,
> Sacred, substantial, never-fading bliss.

PART FOUR

Toward Ethical Excellence

*If your approach is
"I will conquer lust, anger, and greed,"
you will never conquer them,
but if you can fix your mind on God,
the passions will leave you of themselves.
You can never be fully established in morality
unless you believe in God.*

Swami Brahmananda

The Vedantic teachers say, "It is not enough if you perform selfless acts and lead a moral life, it is not enough if you scrupulously perform your duties, but something more is needed; you must attain the highest divine Knowledge and thereby realize the highest goal yourself." Selfless acts and moral practices are only means and stepping stones to the necessary purification of the mind and understanding without which the highest Knowledge cannot by attained by anyone. But the goal itself is the attainment of supreme Consciousness and Bliss. This Consciousness and Bliss are always within us, they are our real nature. Only they are covered with the impurities of the mind. When the impurities are removed the true Self shines forth.

By impurities we mean not merely wrong passions and bad thoughts. Even the so-called good impulses and thoughts are obstacles to concentration and the attainment of the Self, and are hence regarded as impurities. Ethical life insists on the destruction or sublimation of bad thoughts and impressions. But spiritual life insists on the destruction or transcendence of even good thoughts and impulses. Emotions tie one to the mental and the physical planes. Spiritual life means transcending both these planes. That is why a spiritual aspirant is asked to outgrow the so-called conventional good conduct.

Swami Yatiswarananda
Meditation and Spiritual Life

XIV

Should I Compromise?

by Swami Tyagananda

When the desire to lead a moral life comes into conflict with the demands of our secular commitments, the question of compromise assumes tremendous importance. The first question we face is, "Should I compromise?" If compromise seems justifiable or unavoidable, we have to face the next question, "How far should I compromise?" Everyone has to face these questions sometime or other and everyone has to find their own answers. To remain in a state of indecision about the necessity or extent of compromise is to invite internal conflicts which are usually quite painful and debilitating.

Many devotees come to the monasteries of our Order [The Ramakrishna Mission] with this problem of compromise. The problem did not exist for them before they turned seriously to spiritual life. Earlier, they seemed fairly happy and satisfied with the nature of their work and activities. But then they read the lives of Sri Ramakrishna, Holy Mother, Swami Vivekananda and other direct disciples of Sri Ramakrishna, and studied their teachings. They also read and tried to understand some of the ancient scriptures like the Upanishads, the *Bhagavad Gītā,* and the *Bhāgavatam.* All this produced in them the desire to tread the moral and spiritual path, and seek God. Then the problem raised its head. They discovered that many of the things which they simply took for granted earlier were not correct. They found that the demands of a moral and spiritual life clashed with the demands of their secular duties and the pulls of worldly desires and ambitions. The question arose: Should I compromise? It was not easy to answer this question in many cases. Take the case of one business executive. He understands that truthfulness and honesty are the foundations of morality. He also understands that in the course of his work he cannot always be truthful if he has to keep the business running. He cannot afford to close it down; he has got a family to maintain. Should he compromise? Or take the case of an accountant working for a firm. An honest woman, she is ordered by her boss to manipulate the accounts to evade taxes. Refusal can only result in being fired from her job. She has got her old parents to look after at home. Should she compromise with her heart's longing to be honest? There's a clerk serving in a government office. All his colleagues take bribes and he must toe the mark if he is to be accepted by his comrades and not suffer splendid isolation. Should he compromise although he knows that taking bribes is immoral?

More examples are not necessary. Most of us are faced with such moral questions sometime or other. Only two types of people are free from it. One, those who are spiritually illumined. They have gone beyond conflicts. They know exactly what they must do, when and how. They *cannot* do anything immoral. The other type are the out-and-out worldly people whose moral sense has not yet awakened. They too face no conflicts. As in many other cases, here too the two extremes seem apparently alike. All those between these two extremes, that is to say, those who are not spiritually illumined but who have become morally conscious, have to often face the ordeal of deciding whether to compromise or not with the moral ideal.

The Golden Rule

Vedanta teachers have offered a solution which seems simple enough until we try to put it into practice. Swami

SWAMI TYAGANANDA

Turiyananda, a venerated disciple of Sri Ramakrishna, gave this formula to his disciple Ida Ansell:

In matters of opinion, swim with the current; in matters of principle, stand firm as a rock.

In her reminiscences, Ida commented: "He had given me in one moment, guidance for a lifetime."[1] She couldn't have expressed it more beautifully, for Swami Turiyananda's formula is indeed the golden rule for every sincere seeker of God.

One question seems inevitable. How do we decide which are "matters of opinion," and which, "matters of principle?" Usually opinions and principles are so clumsily mixed up that to separate them seems all but impossible. Many times what people consider their principles are really nothing but their opinions. Many times, again, what may be really the principles of others are considered merely their opinions!

Vedanta teachers say that to distinguish between "matters of opinion" and "matters of principle" we first of all need to distinguish between the essentials and the nonessentials. They point out that matters of opinion deal only with the nonessentials and matters of principle deal with the essentials.

This leads to another question: how do we define "essential" and "nonessential?" If anything is essential, it has got to be essential *for* something. What is this "something?" The answer is simple enough: this "something" is the goal of our life. Whatever is essential to attain the goal of our life must be guided by principles, not by opinions. Opinions may change with time, principles don't. Whatever is nonessential to attain the goal of our life is a "matter of opinion." Recall Swami Turiyananda's instruction: "In matters of opinion, swim with the current; in matters of principle, stand firm as a rock." Spelt out through our present understanding, this means we must be firm as a rock in all matters essential to attain the goal of our life. No matter how swift the current, the adamantine rock keeps its place and does not budge. The torrent wants it to

100

move, but the rock refuses to oblige. That is what you and I are expected to do. There should be no compromise whatsoever with the goal of our life and the means to attain that goal. In all other matters, "swim with the current." That is to say, follow the path of least resistance. Be eager to compromise on trifling issues and avoid conflicts and quarrels. What is the point in draining away our energy by quarreling over nonessential matters? The central point of the Vedantic instruction is to utilize all our resources for attaining the goal and not waste them over mundane matters.

The Ultimate Goal

But there are goals and goals. Ask ten people what their goal of life is and most likely we'll get ten different answers. But if we question them further we'll discover that though their goals may appear different, what they are really striving for are not different things. Catch hold of any man or woman in any part of the world and ask him or her point-blank what he or she is really seeking in life. If the person is honest, the answer has got to be, "I want to be happy," or "I want to be perfect," or "I want to be free." No one in his right senses will say, "I want to be miserable" or "I want to remain imperfect," or "How wonderful is bondage!" Happiness, perfection, and freedom can thus be said to be the goal of all humanity. Anything else that is generally spoken of as the goal is really the means which people believe will make them happy, perfect, and free.

People have their own ideas about what would bring them happiness, perfection, and freedom, and that regulates the direction and pace of their lives. Most of them discover, usually when it is too late, that their pursuit of happiness, perfection, and freedom has generated only grief and greater bondage. Vedanta teachers have firmly maintained that the source of all happiness, perfection, and freedom lies within our heart. If we want to be happy, perfect, and free we must connect ourselves to that source. This source is our real Self *(Ātman)*. Self-realization (or what amounts to the same, God-realization) therefore can be the only true goal of human life. It is only this supreme Realization that can bring us unalloyed, unceasing bliss, absolute perfection, and irrevocable freedom. It is in this light that Sri Ramakrishna's teaching: "The purpose of life is to realize God," is to be understood. One important point in this connection is that God-realization is not the *means* to attain happiness, perfection and freedom. God-realization is *the goal* itself, because it is not different from the attainment of happiness, perfection, and freedom.

Given the kind of world we find ourselves in, it is too much to expect that all would accept God-realization as their goal. You can take a horse to the water, but you can't make him drink. Illumined souls have repeatedly taught what the goal of human life is. It is up to us to accept or reject their advice. If we accept it and mold our lives accordingly we become a blessing to ourselves and to society. If we reject their counsel, it only means we haven't yet become ready for the higher ideal and have to pass through more torture and grief before we awaken to the need for something higher.

At this point we must part company with those who reject God-realization as the goal of life. But before we do so, let us mention in passing that whatever be their goal, no matter how worldly it is, let them sort out the essentials and the nonessentials to reach that goal, and apply Swami Turiyanandaji's formula. Their success even in that worldly pursuit is assured. But we must now address ourselves to those who are spiritual seekers. And so the rest of this essay is meant for those brave souls who, whatever their immediate goals may be, have God-realization as the ultimate and supreme goal of life.

Staying True to Principles

What are the "essentials" to reach this goal of God-realization? The answer is not difficult. Everything that would help us to go closer to God is "essential." More specifically, moral virtues such as truthfulness, chastity, charity, selflessness, forbearance, and self-discipline are the essentials. Furthermore, obedience to the instructions of the Guru and the scriptures, faith, dispassion, contentment, and the spirit of service are also the essentials. These things should not be compromised, come what may.

Then there are the nonessentials, which are too numerous and need no listing anyway. Take this simple case. If you want some particular dish for breakfast and your spouse suggests something else, give in. These things are not worth squabbling over. While discussing the political situation of the country with your friends at the tea table don't demand from them absolute agreement with your own pet views—just "swim with the current." To you and me, who are not directly engaged in running the country, politics is only a matter of opinion. Thus, as a general rule, have your peculiarities by all means, but if they happen to clash with the peculiarities of others, don't raise hell with them. Just give way. The nonessentials are *meant* to be compromised.

There is also a third category of things which are not merely nonessential, but positively dangerous as well. These are the opposites of the things listed under essentials. For instance, falsehood, unchastity, selfishness, anger, greed, indiscipline, and so on, are positive hindrances to our goal of God-realization. Keep these things at arm's length. Have nothing to do with them. No compromise whatsoever.

But still the question remains: What if I am forced to close down my business if I don't do what other business people are doing? What if my boss fires me from the job if the accounts are not fixed in the way he or she wants them? What if some unethical union leaders show me the gate if I don't give in to their demands? If I want to be a true seeker of God, to me everything other than the spiritual quest must become secondary. So Vedanta teachers say, hold tight to moral and spiritual values —and if that involves closing down your business, or getting fired from the job, or being scoffed at by your coworkers, so be it.

Suicidal advice, one might say! It is, in a way. If we follow this advice, we are dying to the world and—this is important—unless we die to the world we cannot begin to live in God. When we die to the world, all worldly values become irrelevant to us. When we begin to live in God, life takes on a new meaning. Every time we compromise with the essentials of spiritual life, we *are* committing a kind of suicide. Every time we refuse to compromise with the essentials, no matter what the cost we have to pay for our seeming "stubbornness," we are snapping off one of the many chains that are binding us to the world.

Furthermore, Vedanta teachers assure us that our fears are imaginary. We have nothing to lose and everything to gain by remaining unflinchingly true to the demands of a moral and spiritual life. Swami Vivekananda pointed out that one of the key assets for success in life, secular or spiritual, is conviction in the powers of goodness.[2] Morality and spirituality generate tremendous power against which all worldly powers pale into insignificance. When Swamiji wrote the following words he was echoing his own experience in life:

Truth, purity, and unselfishness—wherever these are present, there is no power below or above the sun to crush the possessor thereof. Equipped with these, one individual is able to face the whole universe in opposition.[3]

Swamiji was keenly aware of the temptation people face to compromise with their principles, so he cautioned:

Above all, beware of compromises. I do not mean that you are to get into antagonism with anybody, but you have to hold onto your own principles in weal or woe and never adjust them to others' "fads" through the greed of getting supporters. Your *Ātman* is the support of the universe—whose support do you stand in need of? Wait with patience and love and strength. . . .[4]

Not for nothing did Lord Krishna assure Arjuna in the *Gītā*: "The doer of good never comes to grief."[5] All that the seeker needs are the three P's Swami Vivekananda often spoke about:

Purity, Patience, and Perseverance—and, above all, faith and love. All spiritual seekers who are true to their principles find, if they are patient enough, that all external hurdles melt away. How exactly this happens is difficult to say. Mysterious are the ways of the Lord. It is as if someone clears the way for the true seeker.[6] And if some hurdles do seem to persist, the seekers find themselves filled with strength to overcome them or to remain unaffected by them.

The problem of compromise, therefore, isn't as complicated as it appeared to be at the beginning of this discussion. What is needed is a correct understanding of the essentials and the nonessentials of moral and spiritual life. The seeker then simply has to remain "firm as a rock," steadfastly true to the essentials, without caring for the apparently negative and inconvenient results that sometimes follow but usually don't. It is seen—and this is attested to by the scriptures as well as by the lives of those who have led perfectly moral lives—that ultimately it is truth and righteousness that triumph, not falsehood and unrighteousness.[7]

As regards the nonessentials, Vedanta teachers insist that compromise is the only way out if there is to be some semblance of peace and harmony in the world. So they advise, "swim with the current."

Vedanta says, study your own life. Find out when you should "swim with the current" and when you should remain "firm as a rock" and then live true to your findings.

FOOTNOTES:

[1] Pravrajika Brahmaprana, "Ida Ansell: Flaming Upwards," *Vedanta Kesari* (March 1991) p. 97.
[2] See *Complete Works of Swami Vivekananda*, (8:299).
[3] *Ibid*, (4:279).
[4] *Ibid.*
[5] *Bhagavad Gītā*, (6:40).
[6] See the Lord's assurance in the *Gītā* (9:22).
[7] *Muṇḍakopaniṣad*, (3.1.6).

XV

Guidelines for Perfection

Swami Chinmayananda

The sixteenth chapter of the *Bhagavad Gītā* describes twenty-six qualities which give us a complete picture of the nature of a person who dwells in the Divine State. These qualities serve as a guideline to all those who long for perfection. To the extent that we are able to change our vision of the world and reorganize our lives along these lines, to that extent can we economize our energies which are required for this higher pursuit. To respect and live these twenty-six values completely is to assure ourselves of the right way of living. They are as follows:

> Fearlessness, purity of heart, devotion to Knowledge, charity, control of the senses, sacrifice, study of the scriptures, austerity and straightforwardness. (*Gītā* XVI:1)

Here we find an exhaustive list of the noble traits found in a person who lives a cultured way-of-life—a life in which these values are practiced in the everyday world. In the enumeration of these qualities, *fearlessness* comes first. Fear is generated in one whose mind is clouded by ignorance. Where there is Knowledge there is fearlessness. By placing this quality first, the divine teacher, Lord Krishna, indicates that true ethical perfection is in direct proportion to one's spiritual evolution.

Next we come to *purity of heart*. No amount of external discipline can possibly provide the student with the positive dynamism which is at the core of all moral living. The *Gītā* invariably preaches a dynamic religion, positive in both its theory and practice. Lord Krishna is not satisfied with a docile generation which only practices passive goodness.

He wants the members of society to burst forth with a positive glow of righteousness, bathing the entire generation with the light of truth and virtue—virtue which implies honesty of intentions and purity of motives. This ethical purity at the level of the heart cannot shine as long as the human mind is turned outward. Only when the mind is lifted up in constant unison with the infinite song of the Soul can it discover the necessary courage to renounce its lower appetites and clinging attachments. Thus, *devotion to Knowledge (jñāna yoga)* is a positive way by which the mind is persuaded to give up all its lower temptations. A mind that is awakened to the serene joys of the Self will naturally never hold on to sensuous objects and their fleeting joys.

The three techniques by which we can develop steady devotion to Knowledge are charity, restraint of the senses, and sacrifice.

Charity must come from one's sense of abundance. True charity springs from a sense of oneness between the giver and the recipient. Unless one is able to identify oneself with others, one will not feel the noble urge to share one's possessions. Thus, charity relates to the ability to restrain one's instincts of acquisition and aggrandizement and replace them with a spirit of sacrifice.

Gifts should be given in accordance with certain ethical norms. For example, we must give only to those causes in which we believe. Charity is acceptable only when it is in agreement with our intellectual beliefs and convictions. Unless we have come to a correct and independent judgment and are convinced of the worthiness of the cause, charity should not be practiced. Every benefactor has the right to inquire into the cause that he is considering patronizing. A miserly giving will not benefit either the giver or the receiver and it is said in the scriptures, "Having come to judge a cause as worthy, give it your entire patronage. Give in plenty, and with both hands." Also, charity must be given with modesty, avoiding feelings of egotism and vanity.

If, through charity, one has developed the ability to detach oneself from one's wealth, then one can also see how controlling the sense organs involves the same spirit of sacrifice for one's subjective life. To indulge the sense organs in the field of sense objects without restraint is to waste precious human vitality.

To keep the mind tuned to the Self in the higher realms of meditation, a subtle yet powerful form of energy is required. And this energy can only be tapped when we have learned to control our senses. Control of the sense organs is impossible without regular prayer and worship, and without this control the spirit of charity cannot be developed. The pilgrimage to Truth is but a wishful dream without the practice of charity and control of the senses. It is interesting to note that each subsequent term in this list is logically connected to the preceding one.

Daily study of scriptural literature, in measured quantities, provides the necessary inspiration to live a divine life. The term *svādhyāya (sva+adhyāya),* meaning self-study, is significant. It suggests that study of the scriptures should be more than just an intellectual exercise. As we study the texts, we must be able to observe, analyze, and understand the truth of what is being said with reference to our own lives. Regular study coupled with consistent practice gives us the strength to live in control of the sense organs. This in turn supplies us with the steadiness in meditation required for realizing the Highest. Conscious self-denial at the physical level when applied in self-development is called *austerity (tapas).*

The "Divinely good" person is *straightforward*—upright in his thoughts, emotions, and general conduct. Dishonesty has a self-destructive influence upon our personality. Actions contrary to one's own true motives result in a deceitful personality.

One who lives this type of life develops a split personality and soon loses his glow of effectiveness.

Truth and Compassion

Lord Krishna now continues to enumerate the mental qualities of the Godly type of people.

Harmlessness, truthfulness, absence of anger, renunciation, peacefulness, absence of deviousness (unmalicious tongue), compassion to beings, uncovetousness, gentleness, modesty, absence of fickleness. (*Gītā* XVI:2)

Harmlessness (*ahiṁsā*) in its spiritual import means never having cruel intentions. Our intentions should not be polluted by even a trace of cruelty or hatred. Harmlessness does not consist so much in never causing physical injury as it does in never contemplating harm of any sort.

Thus, noninjury is a value of life to be applied at the level of our motives. Our motives must be noninjurious and pure. This purity of intention can arise only out of a deep sense of oneness with the Lord's creation and compassion toward all beings, good and bad alike.

Truthfulness (*satyam*) in its essential meaning is the attunement of our mental thoughts to our intellectual convictions, and not just giving verbal expression to our honest feelings. A disparity between thoughts and words creates a habit of "self-cancellation" of thoughts. This impoverishes our mental strength, willpower, and dynamism. Unless we are ready to discipline and marshal our thought-forces to the unquestioned authority of our reason, we cannot realize the unfoldment of our true and divine nature.

Absence of anger is sometimes rendered as angerlessness, which is not quite accurate. A better explanation would be the ability to check waves of anger as they rise in our mind so that anger does not manifest in our actions. It would be unnatural to think that we would never become angry. But no emotion should be allowed to overwhelm us to the extent that we cannot function properly. In short, absence of anger does not mean without anger, but only keeping, as far as possible, an even temper.

Just as we cannot live in a spirit of harmlessness without truthfulness, similarly, keeping an even temper is but a vain hope without the spirit of renunciation. *Renunciation* should not be understood as a running away from life. One who tries to escape from life can never be a champion on the spiritual path. Many have hindered their spiritual unfoldment because of a misunderstanding of this word. Renunciation is not a running away from sense objects and comforts, but rather the intelligent mental attitude of detachment maintained toward the objects around us. A mere understanding of the pain-ridden nature of the world is not sufficient, however. This understanding must be completely assimilated through constant reflection and continuous realization. As we go through life's experiences with intelligent awareness we come to an increasing understanding of the great benefits of detachment. This conviction, gathered as a result of our own personal experience, is the meaning of the term "continuous realization."

This glorious spirit of detachment cannot be practiced in a sequestered place where there are no temptations or challenges. No one can learn to swim on the dry banks of a river. One must learn the art of living in this world fully and enthusiastically with a spirit of intelligent detachment. If a seeker can practice truthfulness, harmlessness, and keep an even temper with a spirit of renunciation, then he will come to experience a great *peacefulness* within.

The next quality is *absence of deviousness (unmalicious tongue)*. The ugliness or beauty of speech is determined by the personality behind it. A shattered personality will seek self-gratification in malicious gossip, whereas an inwardly harmonious person uses soft and sincere speech which echoes the fragrance of his soul. When we speak with softness of tone, clarity of expression, and honesty of conviction we bring a clear picture to the listener's mind with no veiled meanings.

To recognize the infinite beauty of life in and through all of life's imperfections is the secret of enduring tenderness, the *compassion to beings* that is found in all saints and sages. They are able to see goodness in everyone, even in the worst scoundrel.

The next term, *uncovetousness*, means controlling the sense organs from excessive indulgence in sense enjoyments. The average person has an endless thirst for sense indulgence. To remain in self-control without this endless thirst is the nature of a self-disciplined person.

The conduct of such a person will be both *gentle* and *modest*. These are not so much disciplines as they are qualities of a culturally refined individual whose beauty and harmony become evident while contacting the world outside.

Restlessness of the mind and unsteadiness of character are reflected in the activities of an undisciplined person. The body mirrors the condition of the mind. For example, sudden outbursts of activity and exaggerated expressions of the face are all noticed in individuals who have not yet cultivated a noble character and purposeful personality. When seen in children, these may be considered to enhance their charm, but as we grow older real beauty lies in the mastery we develop over ourselves as reflected by our actions.

Absence of fickleness has been explained as not speaking or moving the hands and legs in vain. An extension of this meaning implies an efficiency characterized by promptness and economy of physical energy. Unnecessary exhaustion through indecisive movements and thoughtless exertions are signs of a weak personality. Such individuals may be extremely imaginative but they tend to be lacking in intellectual effectiveness and physical productivity.

Purity and Perseverance

In the next verse Lord Krishna continues to paint the nature of a person of Divine State. With minimum strokes he covers the mental attitude, intellectual calibre, and spiritual glow of such a person:

> Brilliance, forbearance, fortitude, purity, absence of hatred and pride—these belong to one born of the Divine State, 0 Bharatha. (*Gītā* XVI:3)

Brilliance does not mean a glowing complexion produced by good food and ample rest. The glow of spirituality cannot be taken literally as a halo around one's head. It is the irresistible attraction of persons whose light of joy ever shines forth from the innermost depths of their being. It manifests in the brilliance of intellect, the twinkling joy in their eyes, the thrilling fragrance of peace around them, the serene poise in their activities, and the effulgence of their love for all. With abundant energy they serve all and discover for themselves a fulfillment in that service.

The context in which the word *forbearance* is used here does not merely imply an ability to live patiently through the minor physical and mental inconveniences when someone injures or insults us, but the subtle boldness displayed by a person while facing the most powerful opposition and provoking situations.

We cannot always expect favorable circumstances when we daringly meet life. Weak persons often feel dejected and tempted to leave work half done when faced with many obstacles. As a result they miss the chance to achieve their goal when victory may be just around the corner. In order to stand firm in our convictions we require a special energy to ward off this potential exhaustion of our mental and intellectual morale. This inner energy which arises from one's own well-integrated personality is called *fortitude*. Strong faith, consistency of purpose, a vivid perception of the ideal, and a bold spirit of sacrifice make up the source from which fortitude springs forth.

The word *purity* refers not only to the inner purity of thoughts and motives, but also suggests the cleanliness of our surroundings, personal habits, and belongings. Outer cleanliness is, to a large measure, a reflection of our inner condition. Only a disciplined, cultured person can keep systematic order and cleanliness around him. One who aspires to reach perfection will automatically maintain cleanliness both in his relationship with others and his possessions. The scriptures put great emphasis on the need for physical purity because without external purity, internal purification will be but a vague dream.

Harmlessness (*ahiṁsā*) is a virtue that has already been explained in the previous stanza. A similar virtue *absence of hatred* is stated not only for the purpose of emphasis but also to indicate a slightly different meaning. This term means not only noninjury from the standpoint of motives but absence of even the idea of injuring any living creature. Just as a healthy individual could not imagine injuring himself, similarly a true aspirant, in his recognition of the Oneness of all living things, could not even think of hurting anyone else because he knows that to harm another is to harm himself.

Absence of pride means to give up one's exaggerated notions of oneself. This relieves one immediately from many unnecessary agitations and life becomes as light as a feather. Whereas to one who is proud, life is a heavy cross to bear.

The ethical beauty painted here by all the above-mentioned qualities is not with the purpose of giving us the idea of sending the good to an eternal heaven or damning the vicious to a perpetual hell! Ethical virtues are the intelligent means of reviving our exhausted energy and fatigued spirit. By living these healthy values of life, we unshackle our personality from its self-made entanglements. When we worship with true devotion, while employing ourselves in selfless service, practicing self-control and reflection, we bring our mind under control, thus curing the intellect from its false tendencies *(vāsanās)* and our hearts become purified. At this moment we are all acting in accordance with the standards of the times. If we want to lift ourselves to a higher level of existence, we have to change our way of living. Every person undergoes change at each stage of life with old ways yielding to new ones. Similarly, if we want to gain inroads on the spiritual path, change is necessary. Without changing old values, a new dimension of living cannot be achieved. Therefore, a change in attitude and an aspiration to live these noble values is the means to reach the Divine State of Perfection.

Pronunciation of Sanskrit Letters

a	(b*u*t)	k	(*s*kate)	t	no	ś (*sh*ove)
ā	(m*o*m)	kh	(*K*ate)	th	English	ṣ (bu*sh*el)
i	(*i*t)	g	(*g*ate)	d	equiva-	s (*s*o)
ī	(b*ee*t)	gh	(*g*awk)	dh	lent	h (*h*um)
u	(s*u*ture)	ṅ	(*s*ing)	n	(*n*umb)	ṁ (nasaliza-
ū	(p*oo*l)	c	(*ch*unk)	p	(*s*pin)	tion of
ṛ	(*r*ig)	ch	(mat*ch*)	ph	(*p*in)	preceding
ṝ	(*rrr*ig)	j	(*J*ohn)	b	(bu*n*)	vowel)
ḷ	no	jh	(*j*am)	bh	(ru*b*)	ḥ (aspira-
	English	ñ	(bu*n*ch)	m	(*m*uch)	tion of
	equiva-	ṭ	(*t*ell)	y	(*y*oung)	preceding
	lent	ṭh	(*t*ime)	r	(d*r*ama)	vowel)
e	(pl*ay*)	ḍ	(*d*uck)	l	(*l*uck)	
ai	(h*igh*)	ḍh	(*d*umb)	v	(*w*ile/*v*ile)	
o	(t*oe*)	ṇ	(u*n*der)			
au	(c*ow*)					

For information contact:
Chinmaya Mission West Publications Division
Distribution Office
560 Bridgetown Pike
Langhorne, PA 19053, USA
Phone: (215) 396-0390   Fax: (215) 396-9710
Toll Free: 1-888-CMW-READ (1-888-269-7323)